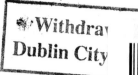

This gripping book will tal ... *of post-partum mood disorders. Importantly, hers is a message of hope, and she describes coming out of that darkness in a captivating, whimsical, enlightening way.*

Professor Gordon Parker AO –
Professor of Psychiatry University of New South Wales,
and psychiatrist Black Dog Institute.

This book is not only a compelling read, but a moving insight into how psychiatric illness affects your mind, body, relationships and the very sense of who you are.

Dr Dawn Barker, psychiatrist & author of "Fractured"

It is fascinating to read of Jen's experiences, documented with brutal and beautiful honesty throughout. A fabulous book that I found impossible to put down.

Bibi Kenedy, Mental Health Clinical Nurse Consultant,
Sydney Children's Hospital

In a graphic account of a terrifying experience,
Jen charts the territory of post-natal psychosis and depression with great courage, vision and wit.

Juliet Stevenson CBE – Award winning actress
and patron of SANE UK

TRIGGER™
The mental health & wellbeing publisher

www.triggerpublishing.com

Theinspirationalseries™
Overcoming adversity and thriving

Rattled
Overcoming Postpartum Psychosis

BY JEN S WIGHT

We are proud to introduce Theinspirationalseries™. Part of the Trigger family of innovative mental health books, Theinspirationalseries™ tells the stories of the people who have battled and beaten mental health issues. For more information visit: www.triggerpublishing.com

THE AUTHOR

Jen Wight is an author, charity fundraiser and feminist. She works for Spitalfields Crypt Trust and has raised millions of pounds and dollars for social justice causes. She is an ambassador for MQ Mental Health and Trustee of the Hyde Charitable Trust.

Jen was the city editor for the Not for Tourists' first ever London guide. She has written columns, reviews and features for a wide range of websites and magazines including *Mamamia, Mumsonthego, Time Out Sydney* and *Third Sector.*

Jen lives in Hackney, East London, with her son, husband and their imaginary pets; Fart, Pamela, Gunnar and Chervil. She is passionate about reducing the stigma around mental ill-health due to her own lived experience of psychosis and severe depression, and that of her sister, who has schizophrenia.

First published in Great Britain 2019 by Trigger

Trigger is a trading style of Shaw Callaghan Ltd & Shaw Callaghan 23 USA, INC.

The Foundation Centre

Navigation House, 48 Millgate, Newark

Nottinghamshire NG24 4TS UK

www.triggerpublishing.com

Copyright © Jen S Wight 2019

British Library Cataloguing in Publication Data

A CIP catalogue record for this book is available upon request
from the British Library

ISBN: 978-1-78956-072-5

This book is also available in the following e-Book and Audio formats:

MOBI: 978-1-78956-075-6

EPUB: 978-1-78956-073-2

Cover design and typeset by Fusion Graphic Design Ltd

Printed and bound in Great Britain by Clays Ltd, Elcograf S.p.A

Paper from responsible sources

TRIGGER™

The mental health & wellbeing publisher

www.triggerpublishing.com

Thank you for purchasing this book.
You are making an incredible difference.

Proceeds from all Trigger books go directly to
The Shaw Mind Foundation, a global charity that focuses
entirely on mental health. To find out more about
The Shaw Mind Foundation visit,
www.shawmindfoundation.org

MISSION STATEMENT

Our goal is to make help and support available for every
single person in society, from all walks of life.
We will never stop offering hope. These are our promises.

Trigger and The Shaw Mind Foundation

the *Shaw* **mind**
FOUNDATION

Creating hope for children,
adults and families

A NOTE FROM THE SERIES EDITOR

The Inspirational range from Trigger brings you genuine stories about our authors' experiences with mental health problems.

Some of the stories in our Inspirational range will move you to tears. Some will make you laugh. Some will make you feel angry, or surprised, or uplifted. Hopefully they will all change the way you see mental health problems.

These are stories we can all relate to and engage with. Stories of people experiencing mental health difficulties and finding their own ways to overcome them with dignity, humour, perseverance and spirit.

New parents don't expect their world to be turned upside down by mental illness, and it can often take them by surprise. Jen's story explains how it happened to her, and what it was like to live with postpartum psychosis. She tells her story in a compassionate and humorous way, which makes it an easy yet incredulous read. But what really makes her story inspirational is her determination to fight for her recovery and to become the best mother she was capable of being.

This is our Inspirational range. These are our stories. We hope you enjoy them. And most of all, we hope that they will educate and inspire you. That's what this range is all about.

Lauren Callaghan,
Co-founder and Lead Consultant Psychologist at Trigger

To my little big sister.

Disclaimer: Some names and identifying details have been changed to protect the privacy of individuals.

Trigger Warning: This book contains reference to vomiting.

Trigger encourages diversity and different viewpoints, and is dedicated to telling genuine stories of people's experiences of mental health issues. However, all views, thoughts, and opinions expressed in this book are the author's own, and are not necessarily representative of Trigger as an organisation.

FOREWORD

One of the things that often happens to new mothers, between 50 and 80% of them, is what's known as "the baby blues". New mothers can feel sad, over-emotional, and weepy at some point in that first crazy week of a baby's life. It is so common that it is considered normal, and is thought to be linked to the huge hormonal changes after birth, combined with the massive emotional upheaval of actually becoming a mother. It doesn't usually last longer than a week. Usually. In my case this period was the start of a long descent into madness and depression.

This story, about the first year of my son's life, is my equivalent of climbing the north face of the Eiger, being kidnapped by jungle rebels, or being wrongly imprisoned for a crime I didn't commit. My version of the baby blues happened on the sixth day of my baby's life. Surviving this day was the third most difficult thing I've ever done. It took all my physical and mental strength – all my coping mechanisms, all my grit and determination. The second most difficult thing was surviving the mind-bending events that happened in the sixth week. And the most difficult ... well, that's revealed in the following pages.

I was one of those new mothers who had no experience whatsoever of looking after a small baby. I'd never changed a nappy or settled a baby to sleep. I'd never bottle-fed one, let alone tried to breastfeed. I naively thought you couldn't take a baby outside for the first six weeks of his or her life, until a kind friend told me that was kittens, not babies.

What follows in this book are my recollections, as accurately as I can remember them given that I was whacked out on painkillers, beside myself with sleep deprivation, and blissed out on being a mother. So take them with a pinch of salt or whatever inert compound takes your fancy. I have tried to be as truthful as I can and have only made additions where it adds to the clarity of the readers' experience. Please note, the names of health professionals, my friends, and some places, have been changed to protect the innocent, as well as the guilty.

Read this book if you are thinking of having kids but are worried about mental health – either yours or someone else's.

Read this book if you've always wondered what people mean when they say that having a child changes everything but have never been able to explain how.

Read this book if having a baby was the toughest, most wonderful thing you've ever done, and you have wondered why there aren't more books about the first weeks of life.

INTRODUCTION

When I was about three, my dad and I were eating breakfast at a large, wooden trestle table outside our holiday rental in the Pyrenees. I was eating butter and honey spread on local bread when I saw something fly by.

'Oh look, Dad, bee.'

'No, Jen, that's a fly.'

'Flies make honey don't they, Dad?'

'No, bees make honey, not flies.'

'What do flies make then? Peanut butter?'

"Funny stuff kids say" is a well-worn trope, and this could easily have fitted that tradition, except for how my dad reacted to it. Responding to his cute little three-year-old, he could have said, 'Ah how funny, how sweet, that isn't right though. You are so silly and adorable.'

But that's not how my dad reacted. He could even have said, 'Ugh, how disgusting, how could you think something so stupid?'

But again, that's not how my dad reacted. He looked at me and smiled.

'What a good guess! It isn't right, but such good use of logic. I can see how you worked that out. Smart girl.'

This then became one of the stories told to me over and over by my sisters, Tania and Jo, and my parents throughout my childhood. The telling of the story was always followed by my mum or dad saying how logical and smart I am. Apparently, I used to ask them to 'Tell the story about the peanut butter' a lot.

That story sums up my childhood. Love, kindness, support, fun, holidays, safety, friends, family. My parents took every opportunity to create in me the belief that I was smart, kind, and funny.

I'm not saying my parents were perfect (they would be the first to admit that) but day in, day out, they did what my mum calls the "daily work" of parenting.

She once told me, 'Every day you have to treat your child as if what they say is important and what they feel matters. This is the daily work of parenting: to make a child feel safe and important. That their feelings – no matter how annoying or irrational – are important.'

This creates a bedrock of security in a child that underpins their personality. Like the way sedimentary rock is formed, layer after layer of sand or silt building up and eventually creating solid rock.

I didn't think about this aspect of my life and upbringing until I was at university in Falmouth, doing my MA in Professional Writing. One of my friends, David, was a mature student like me, and he had travelled to Cornwall with his wife and young daughter. I had babysat for him a few times, so I knew his daughter a little bit. She was a bright, confident, and beautiful child, all huge brown eyes and cheeky smiles.

One day, I was over at David's house hanging out with him and another friend, Joe. I can't remember what we were doing or what we were talking about, but I do remember David looking at us and smiling. Then, in his lilting Scot burr, he said, 'What I want more than anything for my daughter is to give her what you and Joe have.'

Joe and I looked at each other.

'You have this core to you. Something solid and unshakeable. I can tell that you were both loved and treasured as children.'

It moved me so much that the love and care liberally applied to me by my parents was apparent to others.

My mostly idyllic childhood started going off the rails when my middle sister, Jo, hit puberty. Suddenly it was blazing rows and doors being slammed. I was confused by her anger and disgust at my parents, since she was still as loving as ever to me, including me in her life, and telling me stories. When I joined her in the puberty stakes, she would take me to parties and guard me fiercely from the older guys who circled around me (they would beat a swift retreat when Jo, with eyes flashing, told them I was only 14). We would talk for hours about friends, school, life, and which boys I liked. She would let me borrow her cool clothes and the mixtapes that her gorgeous – if mostly silent and intimidating – DJ boyfriend, Otis, made her.

She was a whirl of blonde hair, curves with a tiny waist, chunky silver jewellery. She was beautiful and kind but, looking back, I can see she was troubled. She struggled to be alone and surrounded herself with a rotating cast of friends and admirers. She raged against my parents whenever she felt they were treating us differently.

I was the good one: shy, well behaved, academic. She was wild and rebellious. After doing her A Levels and turning 18, she inherited a small sum of money from my Grandpa Jim. Unlike me, however, she didn't study or take a job; she just worked her way through the money, spending it on drugs, partying, and clothes.

I have so many good memories of her, like the time she and her best friend, Jane, helped me get ready for my first date at a Wimpy on Stamford Hill when I was 13. I had piled my long blonde hair into a bun on the top of my head and was wearing a flared, oat-coloured skater skirt. (I used to have pretty cracking legs before the varicose veins came – thanks, pregnancy!) I remember walking into the kitchen with nerves swirling in my stomach, and seeing the momentarily stunned looks on the faces of Jo, Jane, and Mum. I realise now that it was the first time they saw me as something more than a child. They all jumped up and fluttered around me, touching my cheeks, smoothing my hair and telling me how gorgeous I was, and how my date was going to be blown away. Laughing and teasing me a bit. Trying to ease my nerves.

One Easter weekend, not long after I had met my future husband, Kai, we were going through some old photo albums of family holidays. Mum handed me an envelope containing three loose photos. One showed Jo and I, aged six and three respectively, holding hands in our matching stripy T-shirt dresses.

The other two were of us on holiday in Cyprus. I was 14, she was 17. In the first, we are lying on a bright white sandy beach, asleep, with our heads almost touching on a crumpled beach towel. In the second, she has her arm around my shoulders and is gazing at the camera. I am looking up at her, adoringly. She is so beautiful and calm, with a Mona Lisa smile.

As my mum handed the photos to me, she said, 'You two always did love each other so much.'

That had been the last family holiday we had before things changed. "Life as normal" came crashing to a halt on the 15th March 1990, when I was 15 and Jo was 18. I was sitting in my English class, but I couldn't take in what the teacher was saying. All I could think about was the look my sister had given my mum in the kitchen that morning, burning fiercely with utter hatred and disgust. I have never before (or since) seen such a frightening expression on someone's face.

Jo was standing in the doorway of the kitchen, wrapped in a towel, her long hair dripping wet. Mum was standing at the sink behind me, facing her. I can't remember whether or not they said anything to each other. The look was so bad, so frightening I got up from the kitchen table with my book and my Shreddies cereal, and sat in the lounge, perched on the edge of the sofa, heart pounding, cereal softening in the bowl as I struggled to swallow it down. I don't remember leaving the house, or getting to school.

I later found out that after Jo had gone down to her basement bedroom, my mum had gone upstairs to find that my sister had vomited in the bath. Mum had phoned our GP, who came to see Jo that morning. By the time I was back from school, Jo had been sectioned and was locked away in the psychiatric ward of Homerton Hospital.

There was no history of severe mental illness in our family, and we'd had a secure, loving childhood. At first, they said it was a drug-induced psychosis. But they were wrong. She had suffered a severe breakdown and was caught in the jaws of paranoid schizophrenia. She suffered and suffered, and there was nothing we could do about it. We just had to watch it happen.

We were told that she would likely be out in a few weeks. But instead, she was sectioned, taken from our family home, and locked into the local psychiatric unit for nine months, in what was to be the first of many hospital stays.

For the first few weeks, she slept in a corridor divided up into "bedrooms" by heavy green and brown curtains. She was locked in with people whom I, a fairly hardy Hackney girl, would have crossed roads to avoid. Shouters, screamers, silent rockers. All confused, drugged, and unhappy.

Jo changed overnight, the combination of heavy medication and severe illness stripping her of her personality. I saw how people could have believed in demonic possession. My beautiful sister was gone, leaving in her place a dull-eyed, sedated, occasionally violent stranger who said disgusting things about my mum and dad, treading from foot to foot, pulling her hair tightly into a bun at the very top of her head and refusing to wear her glasses. She became thick and leaden, weighted down with her illness and the body fat that accumulated all around her (a common side-effect of antipsychotic medication, as I would later discover for myself).

Life after that carried on almost the same as it had before, but it was like I had been strapped to a rocket, blasted off the planet and fired into space, then pulled back to Earth where everything was altered. I was burnt and scarred. But only on the inside. Most of my friends who had known my sister all the way through our childhoods ignored what had happened. They never asked me how she was – or how I was for that matter. I don't blame them. They hadn't experienced anything like it and just didn't know what to say. I suspect they didn't want to upset me by asking about it. I had a handful of newer friends who had experienced difficult things in their lives and who seemed to get it; they knew when I needed to talk and when I just needed a hug. I couldn't turn to my older sister, Tania; she had two young kids to look after. I felt so alone. My parents told my teachers, and I was allowed to walk out of class at any time if it all got too much. I would either go and sit in the medical room or find Ms Kelly, a fantastic teacher who listened and supported me at school.

I was doing my GCSE exams at this time, and I'm amazed I passed – I even got some As. Even as I write this, I feel the familiar guilt of "How dare I compare my suffering to hers, of struggling with a few poxy exams when she was in a living hell."

At night, I'd lie in bed on my back and cry quietly, the tears falling sideways and filling up my ears. I remember thinking all those years ago that my beautiful sister had died and that something else was moving her leaden, drugged body around, making it do and say horrible things. I had forgotten how it felt – how easy it was to be unhappy all the time.

I grieved for the rest of my teenage years and into my twenties. I thought it was normal to always need a box of tissues on my bedside table for the nights I cried myself to sleep – it didn't occur to me that it was unusual. I was plagued with survivor's guilt. *How could it have happened to her and not me?* Selfishly, I was terrified that it would happen to me too.

I thought that, since the causes of schizophrenia are either genetic or environmental (or both) and we had a shared genetic and family history (and she hadn't experienced trauma as a child, so it must be mostly genetic for her), logically it must mean I was going to get ill as well.

So, on the 15th March 1993, I spent the whole day crying in bed in my student house and waiting for it to happen. (The 15th March is the date on which Jo was first sectioned, and she was 18 when it happened – as I now was.) I waited for the sky to fall, for my mind to rip loose from its mooring and drag me by the hair screaming and kicking into the nearest psychiatric unit.

Nothing happened.

Thankfully, this fear died away over the years. I dated, started a career, travelled the world, had fun, partied pretty hard, and the pain became easier to bear. I knew I was never going to get married or have kids – the risk of having a child who suffered like Jo was too much. And the lifelong responsibility my parents had? No thanks!

Everyone I ever knew with kids said it was hard, that it changed your life forever, that you had no time to yourself. I believed them.

But I did want a partner, so when I was 29, I told all my friends, 'I'm ready to meet a nice guy. Set me up if you know anyone. And if they ride a motorbike, all the better.'

At that time, I was a massive bike-head, riding my CB250 all around London, loving the exhilaration and freedom it gave me. I could go anywhere without worrying about parking or traffic, without worrying about minicab drivers or horrible men at bus stops. Despite their fear, my parents never once told me they didn't want me to ride a bike. They understood it was my decision, my risk to take. I didn't have a death wish. But looking back I realise that I wasn't that bothered about dying either.

I went on two blind dates with lovely guys but there was no spark. Then, one of my oldest friends said, 'I know just the guy', and that was that. Kai came into my life. For the first year we were dating, I felt like I'd won the lottery. I literally couldn't believe my luck. *He is so good looking, so attractive, so kind, so intelligent, so funny. And he likes me. ME!* I now had a partner who I trusted 100%, and who would support me when the responsibility for looking after my sister came to me and Tania. Things got serious, and after a year, we moved in together.

A few years later, I was hankering after some adventure. I persuaded Kai to quit his job, and we rented out our flat and flew to Australia. I needed to get away from it all, away from the regular updates from my parents about my sister's life and how difficult her illness was for them. This wasn't a conscious part of my desire to leave the UK, but I can't help thinking that, on some level, I wanted to escape. My guilt faded.

My adamance that I would never get married or have kids was also diminishing. More and more of my friends were having babies, and I was amazed at how much I loved these mini people. It was a different kind of emotion, one that was new to me. I guess my biological clock must have finally cranked itself up! I remember the warm swelling of love I had in my chest as I played with a friend's child, repeatedly stacking a set of coloured blocks on a playmat for my squashy gummy companion to knock over with gurgles of laughter. I realised then that I wanted to do it. I wanted kids with Kai.

I was fine. I wasn't going to get ill. I'd been fine all these years. Nothing terrible was going to happen.

The decision was made.

And, though there were some upsets along the way – a feud with Kai's parents, chronic headaches, a potential very early miscarriage and extreme morning sickness – nothing extremely bad did happen. Until six days after my son was born. Then the shit hit the fan.

PART I

Goodbye Bump

Goodbye reflux

Goodbye indigestion

Goodbye heartburn, my old friend

Goodbye hot-foot syndrome, kicks to the colon and
river-dancing on my spleen

Goodbye sciatica, sore tail-bone and needing
three pillows to sleep

Goodbye dizzy head-rush, neck-pulsing,
strangulation-by-neck-muscles feeling

Goodbye racing pulse, and less breath than breathlessness

Goodbye bursting bladder, constipation-blocked diarrhoea

Goodbye not being able to sit up, roll over,
or stand up with ease

Goodbye 'Twins?', 'God, you are huge!' and
'When's your due date?'

Goodbye mood swings, and tearful moments

Goodbye always being hotter than everyone else and
needing to sit down all the time

Goodbye painful pubic bone and random twangs or twinges

Goodbye bump, hello feet, hello ankles

Goodbye bump?

Goodbye holding you close every day, all day

Goodbye guessing which bit of you that is

Goodbye your kicking freaking out Kai

Goodbye bump.

Hello baby.

Hello Boy.

CHAPTER 1

I CAN'T GET NO SLEEP

How can a day be so hard, wonderful, thrilling, amazing, tiring, frightening, weird, cool, confusing, painful, stressful, brilliant, funny, trippy, revealing, sad, happy, fun, and exciting ALL AT THE SAME TIME?

Diary entry, the day of my son's birth.

I had fallen asleep just two hours previously, so I'm pretty groggy when a nurse brings me my son to feed. I know a lot of mums have "just two hours" between feeds in the early days, but I've always been greatly affected by interrupted sleep. My breasts are tight and full, like two over-ripe tomatoes capped with scabbed and bleeding nipples. I attach my limpet-mouthed baby on the least painful of my breasts (the right one) and settle back for the feed. I attach him to the more painful left one, when the right seems empty, wincing as he somehow manages to kick my caesarean scar despite lying horizontally across my body. I wrap him tightly in the standard blue, yellow, and pink hospital blanket and tuck him back into the bassinet. Stumbling into the startling light of the corridor and into the cacophony of the nursery, I hand him over to one of the competent nurses.

This is the last night of five at the private hospital. Private health insurance is a condition of the Temporary Business – Long Stay (or "457") visa that entitles Kai and me to work in Australia for four years.

It's the best money we've ever spent. Trying to come to grips with this tiny, new, jaundice-yellow scrap of life was made so much easier by being in a private en-suite room with magnificent views of Sydney. Three meals a day (plus snacks) helped, too, with tasty homemade broths in tiny cream-coloured bowls and non-mushy veg with everything.

Having your own bathroom also really comes in handy when you're leaking large gobs of blood onto tombstone-sized sanitary towels and lying on another flat absorbent pad to catch any blood that the sanitary towel misses – not to mention the letterbox-sized wound that the baby was delivered through.

But the best thing is having a rotating cast of midwives, physios, nurses, and lactation consultants in the wings who will look after your baby while you sleep (or try to, in my case).

Dr Harper, my obstetrician, is large and kindly with a tired smile on his lips. When he came to check on me post-operation on day one, he said, 'Don't feel bad about putting the baby in the nursery every night; you catch up on sleep.'

I took him at his word and didn't feel bad. Much. I was so overwhelmed and focused on my faulting breastfeeding that I didn't focus on the inkling of guilt. All parents get it, I think.

When my son was born, we were given a marvellous clear-plastic bassinet that doubles up as a baby bath. We wheel him around to breastfeeding classes or physio. And at night when the baby is asleep, I wheel him into the nursery. One end of each bassinet is propped up on its metal frame, so the staff can easily keep an eye on their noisy charges. In the nursery the babies are wrapped tight, like Eskimo offspring, sleeping or crying in rows. Somehow, at any given time, at least half the babies manage to sleep like, well, babies.

Watching the staff in the nursery is a good way to learn that no harm comes of letting babies cry for a bit. These miniature new humans are incredibly resilient. They will not spontaneously combust, die of hunger, or drown in their own tears. It's okay to cry, and yet we are consistently taught not to, almost from the moment we are born. I think this is because it is distressing for parents to hear their babies and children cry. We have evolved to kick into action if our babies are distressed. It activates a very old part of the brain. Crying is the only way babies can communicate, so yes, it is vital to respond to that cry and work out what they're trying to tell us: hungry? In pain? Tired? Need a cuddle? So we spend hours and hours rocking, soothing, and worrying, until we work it out.

*

After handing my son over to the nursery staff, I return to my room and pad about getting ready for sleep. I phase out for a while in a dream-like state, until I realise that, for the last 20 minutes, I've been rearranging the items on my wheelie bedside table (one of those that you can slide over someone propped up in bed). First my eye mask, then glass of water, biscuit, mobile, and call console. The call console is TV remote-sized, and has a volume control, channel changer, and a large central call button. It's attached to the wall behind the bed with a long white cable.

No, I'll need the water nearest and then the call console in the middle, so it doesn't fall off. I step back and survey the table. No, I think I'll put on the eye mask now, but not put it over my eyes. It seems enormously important that I find the correct order before I get into bed ...

A jolt of fear goes through me. *What am I doing? Trying to find the correct order?* But that's crazy. There is no correct order. They are just things on a table. Why am I doing this? What is going on? My chest tightens as the words *anxiety disorder* flash before me in looping handwriting.

*

Earlier the previous day, when the baby was sleeping for long stretches, I started to worry about my medication. Could it affect him? It's a tricyclic antidepressant called amitriptyline. This was one of the first antidepressants developed and, over the years,

23

doctors have discovered that a low dose – too low to work as an antidepressant – has a very beneficial effect on facial pain, headaches, and migraines.

I had been suffering from excruciating headaches for five months and, after trying a number of different treatments (including Botox, agonisingly injected into my jaw and temples), I was referred to a neurologist. He told me what I already knew: that the headaches were caused by stress causing me to grind and clamp my teeth at night. He also told me about a type of amitriptyline but, after checking my age (35, aka desperate for a baby as far as he was concerned), he said, 'It is poison for babies. Poison. So you can't start a family while taking it.'

I remember sitting in his office and staring at his small wrinkled face, furious that he was making such an assumption. Furious that he was right … I had been thinking of trying for a baby. I'd been getting all my jabs up to date and coming off the pill and switching to condoms in preparation – but who was he to assume that I was desperate to have children simply because I was a woman of a certain age?

I went to see my GP and told her that, given what the neurologist had said, I had no choice but to put off trying for a baby because I really needed to try the amitriptyline. But she, marvellous woman that she is, said, 'Let's just double check and ring MotherSafe.' (MotherSafe is a wonderful freephone service run by nurses.)

They told me the risk was very, very low on the dose I would be taking. Did I mention it is too low a dose to work as an antidepressant? Yes? Well, anyway, it is. My extraordinary fear of getting a mental illness was so profound it almost had the power to stop me taking medication that was primarily for a mental health condition. I reassured myself on a regular basis that I wasn't taking them for depression but for headaches, believing the doctor when he said they didn't know why they worked at the low dose, but they did.

They did tell me to avoid a homebirth as the baby might be sleepy and need to be monitored at hospital. As I'd have rather given birth through my ear than have a home birth due to the risk of death or serious injury to the baby or myself, that was no problem. So, out went the condoms and we started trying for a baby.

But now, with my son's little yellow face staying smooth with sleep for hour after hour, I start to worry. I ring MotherSafe again to check that I'm not poisoning my baby with amitriptyline-laced breastmilk.

While I'm on the phone, a woman comes into our room. She is in her late forties and, unlike most of the staff, not wearing a uniform. She has a stern matronly air. She knocks but it's one of those *knock-and-enter-straightaway* type of knocks. Those *I'm-very-busy* knocks.

'I'm Sally,' she says, ignoring the fact that I'm on the phone.

Kai says, 'We are on the phone to Mother Care.'

She looks puzzled.

'MotherSafe,' I mouth.

'Oh, yeah, MotherSafe.'

The very friendly lady on the phone is able to reassure me again and I hang up. I smile at Kai.

'They don't think it should be a problem.'

Sally, on the other hand, does have a problem. 'Why did you ring MotherSafe?'

I explain about the amitriptyline.

'Why didn't you ask one of us?' she asks, standing over us with her eyebrows drawn together. 'They just have The Book, really; they just read out of The Book. We are the ones who know about all the medication. They are going to think we don't know what we are doing. Really!'

'I've always found them very useful,' I say. 'I've had to explain over and over to each shift about the amitriptyline and why I'm taking it. The nurses say, "How are the headaches, dear?" and I have to explain that I take the medication every day, prophylactically, to *avoid* getting headaches rather than as a painkiller for the headaches. That's why.'

She purses her lips as I go on. I'm all too aware of the fact that my abdomen is throbbing and aching.

'They also keep getting the name muddled up with the painkiller I'm taking.'

I had been taking a strong painkiller, but I stopped after just one day; it made me feel so spaced out and trippy that I wasn't sure which end the nappy went on and which end the milk went in. But I don't tell her that. I find out later that this painkiller is in the same family of drugs as methadone and heroin.

Sally leaves the room and returns a few minutes later when Kai is in the bathroom. She has The Book, as well as my notes, and sits down opposite me on the other side of the wheelie table.

'This is all they read out from. Really you should have just asked one of us.' She flicks through the book and finds the drug's brand name (I don't point out to her that all she is doing is reading out from The Book as well). The Book in question is a comprehensive list of all medication and information about risks for pregnant or breastfeeding women.

'Ah,' she says. Her eyebrows unknit and eyes soften.

'You're taking antidepressants.'

'Yes.' I feel a tinge of shame. I felt as though she was judging me for needing medical help with my mental health. I'd always been a staunch believer in my sister taking her medication as I'd seen how bad things got for her when she doesn't, but me? I was different, wasn't I? Every counsellor I'd ever seen had told me I wasn't the same as Jo and there was no reason to believe I would get ill like her. 'But my understanding is this low dose doesn't function as an antidepressant but does get rid of migraines and tension headaches. Both of which I have.'

'So you were having tension headaches?'

'Yes, I was grinding my teeth at night.'

'Why?'

'I had a very stressful situation with my in-laws that was unresolved for many months,' I say. A wave of tiredness breaks over me, and I lean over and start to cry – not full-blown tears, but tired hiccups of sadness. *I really don't want to get into all of this.* 'I started getting excruciating headaches, and I was told that it was because I was grinding my teeth at night.'

She reaches for a box of tissues. Gone are the harsh lines, and The Book lies forgotten in front of her.

'Taking the amitriptyline has made all the difference. I also started seeing a counsellor and have been doing lots of yoga; that really helped, too,' I say, trying to sound more positive.

She murmurs some words of comfort as she flips open the red folder of my notes and reads through. She stops at one point and taps the paper with her pen. The loo flushes and I can hear Kai washing his hands.

'It says here, "anxiety disorder".' She points at the words with her pen.

'What? Where did you get that from?'

Kai comes back into the room, frowning.

'The person who rang you before admission to get a background.'

The day before admission, a woman had rung me to explain what I needed to do on the big day and asked me some background questions. It appeared that the way I had explained my headaches had led her to believe I had an anxiety disorder. Looking back on it now, it seems a sensible link to make as the teeth-grinding was due to stress and anxiety. Who knows, maybe I do have an anxiety disorder?

The power of "IT IS IN YOUR NOTES" really hits me. I'd never been told before that what I had was an anxiety disorder. All it takes is for one person to not listen to you properly, or to not be up to date with current medication, to put something like an anxiety disorder on your permanent record – and on your worry list. The old fear of madness slinks back into the room and takes a seat over my shoulder.

'So, you do have an anxiety disorder.'

'But I'm not taking the amitriptyline as an antidepressant.'

'Nevertheless ...'

She closes my notes and asks about breastfeeding. I explain about all the difficulties I've been having, and she promises to send in one of the lactation consultants.

When she leaves, I burst into proper tears and Kai hugs me.

'God, I've got an anxiety disorder.'

'No, Jen, that is just what someone thought after speaking to you for five minutes.'

This reassures me a bit. But then—

'But maybe I do.'

'I don't think you do.'

'I'm so tired,' I say, and look away.

*

Later that night, Kai is sparked out on the bed, my son is asleep again, and the TV burbles in the background. I'm tidying up the room walking around with my breasts out. Because the room is actually quite chilly, thanks to the air conditioning, I have a wraparound top that I've tied underneath my breasts to give them a good airing. This is to help them heal. I look like a bloated, kinky ballerina. I walk past the dark window and catch something out of the corner of my eye.

I freeze.

On one of the balconies in the building opposite there is the dark shadow of a man with binoculars focused on my window.

I rush to the window to close the shutters, and sit on the chair, breathing fast. I think about waking Kai. But then my son stirs.

He starts to cry, and Kai opens one eye, looking around the room. In the flurry of activity, I forget about the man on the balcony and I don't mention it to Kai in the hours before he leaves and heads for home.

Now, with no husband and no baby here, I'm standing by the bedside table with my hands resting either side of the row of objects. *Something is amiss*, I think. Very amiss. Was someone really looking through the window earlier or was I just being paranoid? Now I appear to have anxiety disorder *and* paranoia. My mental state is in a state. I abandon the sorting and climb into bed. With fear coursing through me, I pull the table over so I can reach the water and the call console. *Calm down*, I say to myself, *calm down*.

CHAPTER 2

PUSH THE BUTTON

I lie on the bed, mask over my eyes, and pull the blankets up to my chin. I'm so tired. I know I must sleep, but my thoughts are racing, tumbling over themselves. *Maybe this is it. This is when it finally happens to me.* My heart is beating fast in my chest. My conscious tries to catch up with my unconscious. *Something is seriously amiss*, I think again. The panic rises in a cold tide from my stomach. *Right*, I say to myself. *Right, you are in a bad situation, things are tough, but you have options, remember. Deep breath. Good. And then another.* Slowly I get my breathing under control though my heart is still pounding.

It is 1.17am.

First, I try Kai's method of going to sleep: to daydream. *I have written a bestselling book – this one you are holding – and I donate half a million pounds to the wonderful charity I used to work for in East London.* I picture the moment I tell Judith, the CEO, that I'm giving them a donation that she and the board can spend on whatever they want ...

Tears prickle my eyes as I imagine how pleased Judith will be, and the difference that the organisation will make to the lives of people in East London living in poverty. But then I start worrying about all the people who might remember an old friendship and call up and ask me for a donation or loan.

I imagine, then, that I will set up a grant-giving foundation called The Wight Winnem Foundation (after myself and Kai respectively). I've worked as a fundraiser for many years, and it is a favourite daydream of mine that I come into a lot of money and am able to set up a foundation to support my favourite causes. I imagine the logo as two overlapping "W"s and setting up the board: Kai, my parents, and two of my closest friends who have many years' experience in the voluntary sector. I imagine that I'll give donations only to pay for fundraisers' salaries, and janitors, and new toilets, and all the other things that most funders won't touch.

God, that would be so great ... that would be ...

I sigh and open my eyes. This isn't working.

It is 1.56am.

Maybe TV will do the trick. I pick up the console, flick on the TV, and scan through the channels. I start watching a budget version of *Alien*. The alien is a disgusting hybrid-being with rows of slime-covered teeth and vicious mechanical arms. It is stalking the humans on a spaceship, and as it leaps out, ripping limbs from bodies, the TV screen ripples and the alien jumps out at me.

I feel the fear again, huge and overwhelming, and I snatch up the console to change the channel. I look at the call button – should I call for help? Am I in trouble?

My thumb hovers over the big square button. *No. I'm fine. There's no alien. Really ...*

I trace the square button with my thumb, but I can't do it. Instead I start flipping through the channels again.

I settle on an early episode of *Charmed*. The actresses look fresh-faced and the film quality is a bit blurry – most probably the first season. *Lame but harmless*, I think. But lame it is not – after five minutes I am gripped by the story of a tiny baby needing to be saved by the Charmed Ones. The dialogue is top notch; the acting, BAFTA-award winning.

Surely it can't be that good, a small voice whispers. *Surely* ... but then the one from 90210 nearly gets killed and I am swept along by the story again. *First seasons are almost always the best, anyway.* I sigh as the end-credits scroll down the screen, and get up to go to the toilet.

It is 2.34am.

Another programme has started: *Absolutely Fabulous*. If I thought *Charmed* was good, then this – this is the best programme I have ever seen! I've always thought it was good, but tonight it transcends all other comedy I've ever seen before. It makes me laugh so hard that I have to press my hand over my caesarean scar for fear of busting a stitch. Saffy is having a baby and Eddie is useless, Patsy jealous. I laugh and laugh until tears run down my face. I text my parents back in London saying all is well (it's their daytime). I picture other choices I might have made giving birth in London with them a 10-minute drive from the hospital. A dull ache of sadness pulls me down, and I feel a sharp pang of homesickness, wishing they were here with me.

As the theme music comes to an end my bubbling high flips down and I am suddenly choked with fear again. Both programmes featured new babies – a bit of a coincidence, I think. It is too weird. And surely Charmed isn't that good, what's going on? Is this madness? Is it happening to me at last?

I sit up in bed, marooned in the centre of the room. I feel the miles between me and Kai asleep at home. I feel so far from home it makes me dizzy – my parents and sisters are thousands of miles away and the gulf is yawning around me.

The darkness swirls around the room, almost like a living thing.

Is this what going insane is like? Am I on the slippery slope down towards the hell of madness?

I cry. And then sob. *Come on, Jen, don't give up; there must be something else you can try* ...

Yoga, I think. *Yoga*. I relax my feet, my feet are relaxed. I relax my calves, my calves are relaxed. I relax my knees ... but my monkey mind jumps out of the relaxation.

God, what is happening to *me*? I'm so tired but I can't sleep. I'm up, then I'm down. *I must sleep; I must sleep*.

I push my eye mask up and check the time.

It is 2.59am.

I try some mindfulness.

'This too shall pass,' I say. 'This too shall pass.' (A good friend of mine told me that, when she was giving birth, she found saying this helped her deal with the pain.)

What shall pass? I think. *Madness? Is this it? Am I going mad? If I'm mad, then I need to ask for help. How can I be so happy and laughing, then so sad all at once? Manic depression, perhaps?*

I start crying in earnest now. Paranoia and doubt wrap their arms about me in the dim light.

I remember Sally waving my notes at me and tapping them with her pen. 'You have an anxiety disorder!'

Down. Down. Down.

It is 3.15am.

I think about ringing my parents, but the vision of them being so distressed upon learning I have gone mad breaks a huge wave of sadness over me, again and again. *I can't go mad; it'll kill my parents*. Well then what should I do? *Push the button*. But I'm scared. *You've nothing to fear but fear itself. Feel the fear and do it anyway, just do it.*

Oh, God, I'm using advertising slogans to cope with this. I must be going mad! *Push the button*. A Chemical Brothers' song goes round my head: *Dur dur da. The time has come to PUSH THE BUTTON. Dur dur da*. I love the Chemical Brothers; I must buy tickets to see them play.

I'M ...

Oh, God, I must be going mad if I'm thinking about buying gig tickets when I've just had a baby! The tears are streaming down my face. All my arguments come around to this one thought: *what am I going to do?* Keep making decisions like *Touching the Void's* Joe Simpson. He nearly died, but he didn't die. All roads lead back to this. Every decision is a good decision.

GOING ...

I've used every trick, every single thing I know to calm myself down, every self-soothing activity, and nothing has worked. I sit with the console in my hand with my finger over the button. The call button is the largest button on the console, square with rounded corners, glowing greenly in the dark. It should say "DON'T PANIC" like *The Hitchhiker's Guide to the Galaxy*. Where is Douglas Adams when you need him?

I sob. *Oh, God.* I touch my hands to my swollen face and rock backwards and forwards.

MAD.

The bed I'm sitting in is a rocket ship about to be blasted into space. The countdown rings out in my ears like the *Thunderbirds* theme tune.

FIVE – This is ridiculous. I laugh.

FOUR – I'm laughing while I'm going mad – so I must be mad.

THREE – Or maybe I really am in a space rocket.

TWO – I know I'm not in a space rocket. I need help. I must press the button.

ONE.

BLAST OFF.

Finally, finally, my face ablaze with tears, I push the button.

CHAPTER 3

IT'S GONNA RAIN DOWN TEARS

The door opens, and a dark figure is outlined in the bright light of the corridor. I can hear two nurses chatting softly at the nurses' station just outside my room and the bing-bing-bing of another room bell going.

'Yes, love?' says the nurse. She stands tall with her arms folded, leaning against the doorframe. Her hair is dark and cut short. It glows, backlit by the fluoro light of the corridor. As my eyes adjust, I can see she has a kind face that is deeply lined in the way only years in the Australian sun can produce.

'I'm having a really hard ...' I sob, still clutching the call console.

She comes into the room and gently closes the door.

'My name is Mel. Can you tell me what is wrong?'

I pause, trying to collect myself. *Just say it, Jen; just say it. SAY IT.*

'I think – I really think that I'm going ... mad.'

The word hangs in the air as the nurse looks at me.

I rush on, 'I'm happy and sad at the same time. I'm frightened, so frightened. I thought someone was staring at me through the window. It's all so weird. I thought *Charmed* was really good when it's quite a shit programme–'

'Don't worry,' she interrupts me. 'This is all totally normal.'

'Normal?'

'Yes; almost all women go through this at around about three days after their babies are born. It's the baby blues. You're exhausted.'

'Yes.'

'And your hormones are plummeting.'

'But I really think ...'

'It happened with me, too, when I had my babies. Long before I started working here. And almost every day in my work here I see women really upset, happy and sad, and having such strange experiences.'

'It happened with you?'

The fear loosens its grip and I stare in wonder at Mel. *This is normal?*

I'm not going mad. My biggest fear, the one that has dogged me all my life, my very worst fear, isn't coming true. Relief floods through me. She is my saviour in a pale green tunic, my small-hours guardian angel.

'I can assure you that it's totally normal,' Mel says. 'I know – that doesn't make it any easier, does it? The best thing to do is have a good cry; turn the sound up on the TV if you are worried about someone hearing you, and just have a good old cry.'

'Are you sure I'm not going mad? I thought the bed was a rocket ship.'

'Yes, really – you're just tired, love.'

'Thank you so much, Mel. Really, really.'

'My pleasure. Honestly, just let it all out.'

She closes the door behind her, and I sit up on the bed with a box of tissues in front of me and let rip.

I cry and cry. My face oozes sadness from my eyes, nose, and mouth. I sob and heave and cry thinking of my parents, my sister, and all the pain. I think about the months of misery with my headaches. All the pain and hurt I've felt since I was 15 comes flooding out, literally dripping down my face and into the steadily growing mound of tissues. I cry for hours, tears washing my face clean until I feel like that river has rinsed away the deep, deep pain of losing my sister, leaving only the shining memories of how much we mean to each other, even now.

Finally, at around 5.00 am, I slip into exhausted unconsciousness, surrounded by a drift of tissues.

CHAPTER 4

WOKE UP THIS MORNING, FOUND A LOVE LIGHT IN THE STORM

I am roused from deep, deep sleep for The Boy's next feed. It is 5.55 am. The nurse bringing the baby in is cheery and doesn't bat an eyelid at my wrecked face and battlefield-bed, strewn with slaughtered tissues. I'm exhausted but feel light and free. It is like the years of worry about my sister, and my own fear of losing my mind, have been washed away by the flood of tears. Apart from my cracked, sore nipples, I feel amazing. I look down at my little son lying awake in his bassinet and waiting for my milk, and feel a surge of happiness and contentment.

I clear away the tissues and prepare myself, lining up a glass of water and another biscuit to keep me going until breakfast. I send Kai a text saying all is going well and that he doesn't need to rush in.

When I half-open the shutters and check out the building opposite, I find that the balcony with the man with the binoculars actually has a large, human-shaped plant in a pot on it. Laughing, I pull the shutters fully open.

The feeling of contentment swells when I bring my son to my breast and he latches on the first time.

This is quite an achievement. "The latch" is the holy grail of breastfeeding and I've been struggling with it right from the start. The very first feed was only a few hours after my operation, and I still couldn't move my legs after the epidural. One of the nurses helped me with the latch, but The Boy was a determined feeder from the beginning and sucked with all his might.

The nurse – one of the few I didn't like – asked, 'Does it hurt?'

(You are supposed to feel a few toe-curling seconds of pain which should fade away if the latch is done correctly.)

'Well, no,' I told her. 'But given that I can't feel my legs, or the gash in my abdomen the baby came out of, I should think nothing would hurt me now.'

'Good, then the latch is okay,' she said, marching out again.

When she returned 20 minutes later, she inspected my breast closely.

'Oh, there's a blister; you must have not latched him on properly.'

'Must I not?'

The blister on one side developed into a crack, closely followed by a crack on the other. Now I am the non-proud owner of two scabbing nipples almost as painful to look at as to touch.

Breastfeeding is truly a biological marvel and I am determined to give my son the best breastmilk known to woman. As well as the amitriptyline, I've also been taking anti-nausea medication for extreme sickness. Add to that the elective caesarean, and I am feeling determined to at least do this bit "right". I know from antenatal classes that your breasts will provide milk when they are stimulated by a baby feeding, and the more stimulation the nipples get, the sooner your milk will come in.

The first few latches are vital as this is when breasts produce colostrum, which is rich in nutrients and antibodies. Also, the nurses know they must start teaching the mother and baby to get the latch right from the start to avoid getting into bad habits. The focus is very much on the latch, rather than getting the baby off your breast at the end of a feed, which was my problem.

The advice given in hospital is to always break the suction of the baby's mouth by 'gently inserting a finger into the corner of his mouth and then disengaging'. Most babies, I found out afterwards, will stop sucking after they have had enough milk, or just when they feel like it. I know other women who have had the opposite problem, with their babies not sucking for long enough to stimulate the breast.

The Boy, by contrast, is what is called a voracious feeder, sucking and sucking long after any early milk is delivered into his hungry stomach. If you have ever seen a terrier holding on to a stick with stubborn ferocity while being spun around, then you will have a good idea of the grip my son had during breastfeeding.

To unlatch The Boy, I have to insert my finger and prise open his jaw, and only then remove my flat nipple from his mouth. By the way, a flattened nipple is another sign of an incorrect latch. But I don't learn that until I am out of the hospital.

*

Back to this morning, and one breast is too sore to use. After feeding for five minutes, the pain is beyond toe-curling in the other, too. I try to release The Boy's mouth using a gentle digit, but he clamps down on my nipple and tears the scab away. My once-beautiful breast starts to bleed. Now neither of my nipples are working as a dispenser of breakfast. I hold the baby away from my body as his face crunches into the cry of a newborn – like a lamb bleating down a tin-can telephone. My calm elation gets up and flies out the window as his cries increase in volume.

I reach for the console, and this time I press the button without hesitation. I hum 'der der dum, the time has come to *push the button*' while the ghost of last night's fear peeps over my shoulder. But then the door opens and the lifesaver, Bernadette, sweeps into the room.

Bernadette is an English nurse with a bosom you could balance a tray on, and an English cut-glass, home-counties accent. Bernadette saw me through my second night, helping me learn the latch with patience while reminiscing about England and Sainsbury's sausages. I remember the contrast of my glowing white breasts and her skilled dark hands as she patiently helped me practise the swooping movement of a tried and tested latch.

'Bernadette,' I say, 'thank God it's you.'

I explain what has happened.

'I think I'm too sore to carry on breastfeeding.'

Bernadette examines my chest with a practised eye.

'These need a rest,' she says. 'I'll get some formula. And the form.'

She rolls her eyes at me sympathetically, and she pulls the door shut behind her. I walk around the room jiggling The Boy as his cries build and build.

The form, as it turns out, is a waiver I have to sign before I can get the formula. I have to sign that I am aware that using formula could negatively affect my ability to breastfeed in the future. It's just formula, not formaldehyde, but I imagine a lawyer somewhere has worked out that the hospital may get sued by a frantic mother who blames the nurses for using formula when the mother was at a low ebb. Or maybe they already have.

'I'm sorry about the form but we really do have to get it signed.'

'I don't mind. There's no way I could do more breastfeeding right now.'

'We'll make sure you have someone show you how to express, so you can rest your nipples.'

I imagine my nipples going off to a rest home for battered body parts as she shows me how to hold The Boy and bottle-feed. Peace descends on the room once more.

'See, you're a natural,' Bernadette says as she glides from the room like a galleon in full sail. As she leaves there is a knock at the door. The first of many. It is breakfast.

'Lovely morning,' I say to the orderly as he places the tray on my table. He looks everywhere but at me and, as he closes the door behind him, I realise I've tied my wrap under my breasts again and my battered beauties are on display. And I just don't care.

CHAPTER 5

PUMP IT UP A LITTLE MORE

When Kai arrives, I'm tucking into my breakfast of cornflakes, tea, and toast while The Boy coos in his bassinet.

It is 7.34am.

'Had to start him on formula as my boobs are wrecked,' I explain. 'I've had such a strange, awful night, really weird.'

Kai constructs a bacon sandwich from my leftovers as I finish my tea.

'What happened? Was it The Boy?'

'He was in the nursery, but still I only had about two hours of sleep, and I'm knackered.'

'Two hours? Why?'

The door opens, and a kindly lady with a face full of wrinkles and a sweep of white hair steps in.

'Flowers!' she bellows at the top of her voice.

The flower ladies are all volunteers at the hospital making sure any flowers are well looked after. She looks around the room.

'Ah still no flowers,' she says, looking at me. Her wrinkles have rearranged themselves into a map of concern.

We smile at her and I say, 'Nope, no flowers,' and she pulls the door shut behind her.

On our first day, she'd shouted 'Flowers!' and looked around the room for any trace of a pale petal or glossy leaf. In her world, a new mother without flowers is like an elephant without a trunk. It just isn't right. Almost as if flowers are an essential part of the birthing process, perhaps delivered by the mother in between baby and placenta.

'I should have just bought some flowers,' says Kai. 'Just to keep her happy.'

'Do you remember we went in the lift up to the maternity ward with her?'

'Oh, yes!'

She'd had vicious-looking shears and secateurs laid out like surgical instruments on a metal trolley. 'I hope she doesn't do your delivery,' Kai had whispered to me.

'So, what happened last night?' Kai asks now.

'After you went–'

There is another knock at the door, and Dr Harper enters the room.

After the greetings and hellos, he says, 'Let's check your wound then.'

I roll onto the bed and inch my tracksuit bottoms and knickers down. The wound glares up at him, red and angry looking, fringed by pubic stubble.

The most pain I experienced on the day of my son's birth was when one of the nurses shaved the top inch of my pubic hair triangle. This was more painful than the cannula being inserted into the back of my hand, the epidural injection into my spine, and way more painful than the careful slicing of six layers of tissue to break into my womb.

I'd heard of women getting the whole area waxed and thought this was due to vanity or shyness about showing a room full of people their muff. I'd thought, *Well, the doctors and nurses will see more vulvas in one week than most people see in a lifetime. They're not going to bat an eyelid if I have hair down there*. But, even though I knew the cut would be under my bikini line, I hadn't put two and two together and dealt with it myself.

'Do you have pubic hair?' the nurse had asked me an hour before the operation was due.

'Yes,' I said, thinking, *well ye-es, since I'm over 14 and have managed to get myself pregnant, I think you can safely say I have passed through the trials and tribulations of puberty*.

When she started shaving me, it seemed to go on for hours as she scraped and scraped with a razor so blunt it would make a banana look like a deadly weapon. Kai sat squirming in the corner of the room, throwing me looks of mouth-twisting sympathy. While the nurse scraped my hair away, I pondered the subjective nature of pain. I think my jittery nervous state made the pain of my skin being dragged along under the blunt blade much worse. Despite how long she spent on the task, though, she somehow managed to leave a rash of angry stubble rather than a clean shave, and this was to cause me more pain when the dressings were removed later on.

But that was on day one. Back in the room with Dr Harper, he closely studies my wound and then looks up at me.

'Good, good,' he says.

Another face, this one with short fair hair and pale eyes, pops around the door and sees the doctor.

'Oh, I'll come back later,' she says, shutting the door.

'Thank you, Doctor, for everything,' I tell him, and he smiles as I hitch up my trousers.

We all look at The Boy, asleep in his bassinet. Dr Harper is speaking but I can't stop staring at the little monkey-faced baby who is actually mine. I still can't believe it. We actually have a baby!

'Intercourse,' says Dr Harper.

'Er?' I say.

'This is going to sound strange, but I have to let you know that you can still get pregnant if you have unprotected sex. It doesn't matter that your periods haven't started again. It is really important that you know this.'

'Sex?' I scoff. With a barely healed slash inches away from my foof, tits like unripe rockmelons, and a tiny newborn to look after, I can't think of a time when I have felt less like having sex. Well, apart from one of the worst bouts of cystitis I'd ever had while on a camping holiday in Wales.

I look at Kai.

'Sorry, darling, I don't think I'm quite in the mood.'

'Fine by me,' he says.

The doctor laughs and says, 'I bet that's the first time that's happened'. Then, in a radical topic jump, he asks, 'How is the constipation?'

'Oh, much better thanks. I did a poo yesterday.'

You really don't mind discussing your poo with a man who has cut you open, reached in and pulled out your newest family member.

The day before, the doctor had advised me to take anti-constipation medication as I still hadn't "opened my bowels". This advice had been echoed by a woman sitting next to me at a settling class in the hospital, who had whispered hoarsely into my ear, 'Make sure you don't get constipated – it's agony! Drink lots of water.'

Constipation is the enemy of pregnant women and new mothers. When I was pregnant, I was taking medication to help with extreme morning sickness, which made me constipated. I was firing out painful, rabbit-poo-sized pellets into the bowl.

In between kneeling on the bathroom floor with my arm draped over the toilet seat, vowing to start a campaign to abolish the term morning sickness, and trying not to get caught in the splash-back following a particularly violent burst, I'd also found the time to ring Dr Harper.

'I can't push the baby out, can I?'

'No,' he'd told me, 'but get yourself some fibre supplement.'

The supplement entails mixing the orange powder with water and drinking it quickly before it has a chance to solidify, and it got things moving admirably. But I did find it very disconcerting one day when I threw up an oesophagus-shaped blob of orange goo. *Ah, the joys of pregnancy ...*

Back in the hospital, Dr Harper kisses my cheek and shakes Kai's hand as he leaves us.

'Can you imagine having sex now?' I ask my husband incredulously.

Kai laughs and gives me a careful hug.

'So, tell me about last night,' he says.

'I need a shower before the next person comes in. We need to check out by ten o'clock.'

I relax in the stream of hot water, the room clouded with steam, but all too soon I hear the door again.

'She's in the shower,' Kai is saying.

I dry myself cautiously, dabbing at my wound and scabbed nipples to make sure they are dry. I pop my head around the door.

'All clear?' I ask. Kai nods.

Getting dressed, I carefully pack away my battered breasts into my black maternity bra tucking a reusable breast pad into each cup. Kai has started clearing the room, carefully and systematically packing my clothes and The Boy's things into a bag.

In our relationship, Kai, with his amazing organisational skills, is the packer. I found out later that he'd spent a couple of hours the night before using a tape measure to measure all the onesies we had and then sorting them by size. It seemed like a perfectly sensible thing for him to do at the time.

The door opens again. It is the bright, wonderful Susan. She has shiny brown hair, pink cheeks, and a round, smiley face.

'How's it going?' she asks.

I tell her about my trials with breastfeeding and needing to learn how to express.

'I'll go get a machine,' Susan says.

Moments later she is back, pushing a creamy-yellow machine on wheels. It has two clear-plastic tubes snaking out the top and two dials on the front. She also has what looks like the contents of her Tupperware drawer.

'It's fairly easy once you get the hang of it,' she explains as I unpack my boobs again and get ready to hook myself up to the machine. The scab on one nipple sticks to the breast pad, making me wince as it comes off when I peel away the pad.

'Ouch,' winces Susan. 'If you put a little dab of nipple cream on before you next put on your bra, the scabs won't stick.'

Susan patiently explains how the machine works and I give it a go. It has two speeds: one to stimulate the let-down, which gets the breasts starting to work, and a faster speed to actually pump the milk out. Susan attaches a funnel and a clear-plastic bottle to the end of one of the plastic tubes. She shows me how to attach the funnel to my breast with the nipple in the middle of the tube. Once the faster speed starts, my nipple is sucked into the tube in a pink cylinder of flesh, and the flared cup of the funnel is stuck onto the surrounding breast.

'You can adjust the power here,' she explains as she shows me. 'And the idea is to have it just below the painful point.'

'My nipples are quite painful all the time,' I say.

'Ah, okay, then we'll have it on a low pressure to start with.'

I can see little spurts of milk shooting out of invisible holes in my nipple and trickling down into the plastic bottle. One of the more painful things that can go wrong when you are learning to breastfeed is mastitis. Luckily, this fate didn't befall me, but many women get mastitis at some point, and it is usually caused by a blocked milk duct. When you are first learning to breastfeed, you're taught to massage your breast and watch for lumps; these are early warning signs of a blocked duct.

'You can hire these machines from your local chemist,' Susan tells us. 'You alright for now? I'll be back when you've finished this to take out your stitches.'

When she has gone Kai looks at me.

'I'm a human cow,' I say, and he laughs as we hear yet another knock on the door.

CHAPTER 6

I HOPE MY LEGS DON'T BREAK

It is 8.57am. The door opens and a tall, athletically built woman with short fair hair and pale green eyes strides in.

'My name's Jackie,' she says. 'I'm one of the lactation consultants here.'

She stands looking at me as I am attached to the pumping machine.

'So, I understand you are having trouble breastfeeding,' she continues, looking at the folder with The Boy's notes. It gives details of nappies and feeds, which we've been filling in religiously.

'I've had to stop altogether this morning as my nipples are in a terrible state.'

'Were you having problems with the latch? I see you've had Bernadette and Susan. They're usually really good at teaching people the latch.'

'Yes, they were great, but he just sucks and sucks. Whenever I've asked for someone to watch the latch, they say it's fine, but by the end my nipple's even sorer and is squashed flat.'

'Maybe he was slipping off your nipple during the feed?'

'Maybe.'

'You need to reattach if that happens.'

'How can I tell?'

'Because it hurts.'

'But it hurts all the time.'

'Ah, well, it hurts more.'

She falls silent as The Boy wakes and starts protesting. Kai picks him up and starts walking around the room in the centuries-old jigglewalk that most parents are arm-achingly familiar with.

'Anyway, I can tell you about formula feeding while you rest your breasts, and then you can get back to breastfeeding in a few days.'

I'd heard about "the Breastapo", but hadn't encountered a member yet. These are midwives and nurses whose keenness on breastfeeding somewhat overwhelms their ability to be kind and considerate. Jackie was the closest I'd come to Breastapo; she just assumed that I'd go back to breastfeeding, and I was so convinced that I would breastfeed, had wanted it so badly, that it was easy to go along with her.

'So first you need to work out the dose, which is the amount of formula that the baby needs.' I drift off for a second. Then it seems like she is saying, 'This is baby's weight times his weeks of age. Then add your birthday, your weight, pi, and then Planck's constant. If the month has a "u" in it then you need to double the number you first thought of, and then highflip the dingkerton squash-a-squiggy. Then you klingfarf the first feed of the day. It is really important that you remember to toddlewhap-burger the highflip ... and never forget to maintain good bottle hygiene.'

'Sorry I'm finding this really hard to follow. I didn't get much sleep last night. Can you write it down?' I ask Kai.

She goes on explaining and Kai frowns with concentration as he scribbles in his notebook. I turn off the breast pump and gently break the suction to remove my poor breast from the funnel.

'I can see you've got the hang of the breast pump, anyway.'

'Yes.'

'So, you see, it's really quite simple,' she says to Kai as she leaves the room.

'Did you get any of that?'

'Some,' replies Kai, frowning at the notebook in his hand.

I shake the bottle to see how much I've managed to express. A small amount of the precious white liquid sloshes around in the bottom.

'I really want to breastfeed,' I say, and my bottom lip trembles. Kai comes over and folds me into his arms as I start crying.

'You will, you will,' he reassures me.

Susan knocks again and pops her head around the door.

'Oh, sorry.'

'I'm just so tired,' I sob, blowing my nose.

She gives us a sympathetic, lopsided smile. 'I was going to take your stitches out. Shall I come back?'

'No, now is fine.'

Wiping my eyes, I hop back onto the bed and roll my trousers down again.

'I see some of your hair has grown back,' Susan observes.

She's not wrong. The dressing around the stitches is stuck to the short hairs around the wound. She inches the dressing off and I wince as it pulls and drags against the wound and surrounding puckered flesh. Then she cuts the blue thread and gently eases it out of the scabbed and red skin.

'Sorry about this,' she says.

It is 10.29am.

*

I'd had an elective caesarean. The Boy had been breech for most of the latter half of the pregnancy and, given the size of his head

(97th percentile) and broad shoulders, Dr Harper recommended a C-section. He said that getting the body out and then getting the head stuck was a situation we really wanted to avoid. I'd laughed and said, 'Ouch.' He'd replied, 'The baby will have an increased chance of death or cerebral palsy.' *Decision made, then ...*

As it turned out, the caesarean went without a hitch and the birth itself lasted no more than three minutes. The whole procedure took less than an hour. The pain was non-existent, but there were some bizarre occurrences ...

I was lying in the anteroom of the theatre, waiting for my turn. The room was small, but fitted the large hospital bed comfortably, and it had white cupboards lining one wall. Kai and I had just been laughing that the sign on one of the cupboard doors had a list of contents including cocaine.

'Cut me up a line,' I said to Kai in my best Ray Winston accent.

The doors to the theatre had porthole-type windows and through one I could see the infrared lamps on the ceiling. Reflected in the round redness of one of them I could see a neat and tidy lady garden. I was just about to say to Kai, 'Oh, look, I can see ...' when a scalpel hove into view and started cutting. I turned my head and buried it in Kai's arm.

'What is it?'

'I can see a scalpel cutting!'

'Can we go with the stork option?' he joked.

When it was my turn, they sat me up on the bed so that I was leaning forward on my bump. Kai was gripping both hands. I was so giddy with nerves and weirdness and the drugs they had me on, that I barely felt the injection going into my spine. I lay back with my lower half shielded from view by green sheets. The surgeons chatted about golf while they sliced me open.

'It's like being wrapped in snow,' I said to anyone who was listening to me.

'You okay?' asked Kai.

I could feel them reaching in for the baby.

'It's like I'm a handbag and they're reaching around for their lost keys.' We both giggled.

'Camera time!' called the nurse when they pulled The Boy out.

As they carefully sutured the layers of flesh that made up my abdomen, I could hear two nurses counting the instruments to make sure none had been left inside me.

'They sound like the improbability drive of the Heart of Gold counting down to normality,' I said. One of the reasons I love Kai is that he knew exactly what I was talking about. (And for those of you who don't, that's another reference to *The Hitchhiker's Guide to the Galaxy*.)

But back to Day Six.

*

It is 11.03am. There is another knock and the paediatrician comes in. She is a young, Asian doctor with straight black hair and wide, intelligent eyes. She lays The Boy on the bed and starts to check him over, listening carefully to his chest and gently rotating his legs.

'All okay,' she declares, and Kai and I simultaneously let out our held breath.

'Great,' says Kai.

'So, you had an elective caesarean?' she asks. 'Why was that?'

I tell her about what Dr Harper had said about the size of The Boy's head and shoulders and the increased risk of something going wrong at the birth.

'As it turns out,' I say, 'he wasn't as big as the scans suggested, but his head is in the 97th percentile.'

'Yes, he does have a large head.'

We all laugh, and she looks up at us.

'Well, you both have large heads so it makes sense.'

I catch Kai's eye but have to look away quickly so we don't smirk.

After the blur of visitors and door-knocks, we are finally ready to leave. Kai goes down to bring the car around to the entrance and I wait in the nursery with our tiny little one in the bassinet. A grandpa and grandma are sitting cooing over an even tinier baby, fresh from the egg.

'Congratulations,' I say.

'Our new grandson,' says the woman, eyes bright with tears. 'His mother is in recovery.'

Kai tells me he also waited in this room with The Boy when he was less than a few hours old, waiting for me to come up from recovery. One of the nurses gave him tea and biscuits. He said it was the strangest hour of his life, sitting waiting with the barely born being, still wearing his blue scrubs and a label saying *Dad*.

I feel a spangle-bright spark of fearlove for The Boy – filled with the hopes and fears of a first-time parent – and am just picking him up for a cuddle when the text comes.

Ready.

I put The Boy back into the bassinet and wheel him out of the nursery past the nurses' station.

'We're off then,' I tell them.

'Great,' says one of the ladies behind the counter.

'Good luck,' says the other.

'Could you say thank you to Bernadette and Susan. You've all been so wonderful, thank you.'

'That's lovely. Will do.'

I stand in silence, looking at them.

They look back at me.

'So can I just go?'

'Yes, your husband has taken care of everything.'

'I can just take him?'

They both laugh. 'Yes, love.'

I can't believe they are just going to let us take the baby. Us and a baby. *Us. And a baby.*

I feel like I'm surrounded by a force field that warps the corridor as we walk down to the lifts. I hum The Police's 'Walking on the Moon'. *Dant da narrrr*. The walls pulse and shimmer as though through a heat haze.

Down at the car, Kai slips The Boy into the car seat.

'His first drive,' I say.

'His first everything today,' replies Kai as he sets off. The force field is still surrounding us, but it doesn't keep the cars away.

'They are so *close*. So *fast*,' I say nervously.

Kai doesn't respond, instead focusing all his attention on the road ahead. Cars seem to swerve and race past. The roar of traffic seems deafening. I remember a friend telling me that he felt like reaching out and pushing all the other cars away when he and his wife brought their daughter home.

It is a bright and sunny day. Everything seems brand new, freshly minted. The shop windows along Military Road twinkle, as if just polished. I catch Kai's eye in the rear-view mirror.

'Everything is so ... different,' I say.

He nods, then refocuses on the road. The Boy starts a hiccupping bleat and my heart lurches. Now we have to deal with him on our own, with no help. How are we going to cope? How am *I* going to cope? I give him my thumb to grip and the bleats subside.

When we arrive home, we find two builders working on the awning outside the block's front door.

Kai had warned me this was likely to happen. About a year and a half ago the building had some work done on it, replacing the railings and resurfacing the walkways. At the time, they had taken down the wooden awning but never replaced it. We had been half-heartedly nagging our lovely landlady about getting it put back up for the last year or so.

'Today of all days,' I sigh. 'Nice.'

The two builders greet us as we huff up the stairs.

'How you doing?' One of them asks with a strong Welsh accent. His face is all smiles, topped with wavy fair hair. He has a large tattoo on his upper arm.

'Oh fine,' says Kai. 'Here is our son.' He holds the carry-cot out for inspection.

'Where are you from?' I ask. 'Wales?'

'Yes, South Wales.'

'Ah, him too,' I tell him, pointing at Kai. He's half Welsh – Swansea born – but having grown up in Norway is a little bit more 'Wegian than Welsh.

'I'm Donk,' he introduces himself and holds out his hand to Kai.

'How funny, both from South Wales and now meeting in New South Wales.'

Donk grins even wider and I leave them to chat about rugby as I take The Boy inside.

'We'll really try to keep the noise down,' says Donk, and the other silent builder nods in agreement. And they really do. If it is possible to hammer quietly then these men – two of the most considerate builders in Australia – manage it.

CHAPTER 7

NOTHING CAN COME CLOSE

It is 12.57pm.

As we wander about the flat, dazed and confused, all we can hear from the outside is the dull *tap tap tap* as they go about fixing the problem the other builders had left behind.

I sit on the sofa with my son next to me in his carry-cot while Kai brings me a large bowl of Shreddies.

'You lucky thing,' I whisper to the baby. 'You are going to get some Shreddie-flavoured milk.'

I love Shreddies; my parents had sent them over specially from the UK. I once had a very vivid dream that I got one plated in gold and wore it on a chain around my neck. They are my go-to breakfast cereal in all manner of situations.

I flick on the TV and *Charmed* pops up on the screen. A slight prickle makes its way down my neck. *Charmed again?* I think.

'That's weird,' I say. '*Charmed* was on the TV last night.'

Kai smiles at me, but his eyebrows are drawn together in confusion. 'Why weird?'

'I've got to tell you a bit about last night. I couldn't sleep and so many weird things happened.'

'Like what?'

'I really thought I was going mad. I'm so tired.'

He comes over and gives me a big hug.

'Well, why don't you tell me more about it after you've had a sleep? You need your rest. All I need to do is pop to the chemists to borrow a breast pump. Will you be alright with the baby for 20 minutes or so?'

I look at our son in the carry-cot, his face smooth with sleep.

'Sure.'

I watch *Charmed* and am again struck by how good the programme is. It's really amazing! *I must still be sleep-deprived*, I think. I look at my watch. Kai has been gone for five minutes. The baby stirs in his cot.

Don't wake up. Don't wake up. I can't cope with you on my own. I stare down at my son, totally terrified. I suspect all new mums have this experience as the enormity of their new responsibility dawns. It's difficult to know what exactly I'm scared of. He's so much more important than me, so unknowable, and so many things could go wrong. It's like handling a baby-shaped hand grenade that might explode at any minute.

I start crying. *Why is Charmed on again? It's just too much of a coincidence.* I look at my watch. Six minutes.

Deep breathing, deep breathing. I try to slow my breath and calm myself down. My eyes flick to my watch again. Damn. Only nine minutes. I turn the TV off and start pacing the room. The tears keep bubbling up. I thought I'd got through the worst last night, but here it is again – the terrible fear, the same as last night. *This is it. I'm really going mad.* I sob silently, not wanting the neighbours to hear me.

After what seems like five hours, Kai comes back from the chemist.

'What's wrong?' he says.

'I really think I'm going mad. Really. Really. I nearly did go mad last night. It was so awful. I couldn't press the button and–'

'Sweetheart, you're just really tired.' He bundles me up into his arms and guides me to the bedroom. 'You just sleep now.'

He is kneeling by the side of the bed, an arm around my shoulders. I feel the warm solidity of him by my side, his strong arm holding me tight. The knot at my throat loosens slightly.

'So you don't think I'm going mad?'

'No, but, Jen, no matter how many times I tell you, it doesn't matter. You need to believe it yourself.'

I gaze at his handsome face, his eyes crinkled in a tired smile. He is right. I can trust him. Smiling back at him, I relax back onto the pillow and my eyes droop.

I drop into sleep, but I am still awake. My body is heavy with sleep but not my mind. My eyes are closed and my arms and legs are weighted down. But my mind won't let go. My leg jerks and I lie there waiting for my brain to switch off. My arm jerks. I will myself to sleep but my mind is blinking and beeping. It will not let go of the awakeness.

It is like I'm lying submerged in water, and it's lulling me to sleep, but I have a small straw in my mouth that's connecting me to the awake world. *This is what is must be like for babies when they are overtired.* I'd heard this expression before but never understood how you could be really tired but not able to go to sleep.

I can hear Kai when he comes in to check on me, imagining the smile on his face when he thinks I'm asleep. My body is so heavy that I don't think I could sit up if I wanted to. The minutes stretch and yawn around me. The world whirls about my head; my single point of focus is where my body meets my mind. I feel nailed to wakefulness at this point. I wait for sleep. I wait. I wait.

*

I must have finally drifted off to sleep because the baby's cries wake me up. I lie on the bed staring up at the ceiling with my breasts bursting with milk. Milk has leaked onto the sheets and my nightie. I can hear Kai talking to the baby and I drag myself up out of bed.

It is nearly six o'clock.

Kai hugs me as I stumble from the room. Everything is crystal clear and shining bright. Out the window, the blue water of Sydney Harbour is wrinkled by small waves. The small stretch of sand across the inlet is in sharp relief.

'Did you sleep okay?' asks Kai.

'Sort of – it was weird.'

'That's your word of today, "weird".'

'Well, it has been.'

'Are you feeling any better?'

'Yes, much,' I reply, turning the kettle on. I must have got some sleep at least and the world seems more normal again.

'Tea?'

'Lovely.'

Kai is giving the baby his bottle and I sit down on the sofa. He has set up the pumping machine on the windowsill to the left of the sofa. He has also put together a feeding station with three jam jars filled with nuts and raisins, chocolate biscuits, and crackers, and has filled up a large bottle of water and placed it next to a glass.

This is typical of the kind and thoughtful things he does for me. I reach over and give him a grateful hug.

'Time to get pumping,' I declare.

Untying my top, I carefully peel my scabbed nipples away from the breast pad. I am relieved that the scabs stay where they are. As my nipple gets rhythmically sucked in and out of the plastic tubing, I try to explain what had happened the night before. Kai listens in silence.

'That does sound weird.'

'See, I told you!'

After pumping both breasts, I've managed to express 30ml of milk, which I pop in the fridge. I have a light buzzing feeling, chilled and mellow. Kai has placed the baby in his bassinet, which has been moved into the living room. I look down at our baby, who is gazing up at me. *This is my baby*, I think. *I grew him. Not long ago he was inside my body. Now he is out in the world.* A feeling of euphoria rushes over me.

'I think breastfeeding is getting me high,' I say.

Kai tells me the Norwegians have a phrase for it: *ammetåke*. It literally means "breastfeeding mist".

He has defrosted one of the meals I'd made in bulk and frozen the week before our son was born. The table is laid with glasses of water and candles. Still feeling a little overwhelmed, I look over at him.

'You are so wonderful,' I say.

'I know.'

We laugh.

'I love you,' I tell him fondly.

'I love you too.'

'We have a baby.'

'I know.'

'Us.'

'I know.'

'So weird,' I say for the final time that day.

The rest of the day passes uneventfully. We settle our six-day-old son for sleep and he is sparked out by seven o'clock. We eat dinner and watch a bit of TV. We sit in bed and read before we go to sleep. *Phew.* We are getting the hang of things. Everything is going to be alright. And everything is alright. Until week six.

CHAPTER 8

WHERE IS MY MIND?

Much less tired today but still not totally with it. In between pumping the right and the left boob I picked up my glass of water. Very thirsty. But instead of drinking it I offer it to my right breast. Oh dear.

My diary entry.

In the first heady weeks of our son's life, I am so, so happy – most of the time. It felt like the burden of 22 years' worry and fear of going mad like my sister had been rinsed from me by my marathon crying session in the hospital, bringing in a tide of happiness and positivity. I love my son so much that it feels like an explosion in my chest whenever I look at him.

This is it; now my life can begin again. Wow.

It's as if a big chunk of my brain had been busily occupied with maintaining the draining level of fear and anxiety, but that fear and anxiety is now gone. That bit of brain's suddenly found itself with nothing to do, and the sensation is weird. I think I must have got so used to the work of worrying that I didn't even notice that the drain was happening; it just *was*. Either way, I'd thought that time was behind me.

Now what?

After a few moments of shock, my brain sets about carrying out a combination of useful new tasks: my spelling improves;

I stop losing things around the apartment; I'm a better gardener and I can suddenly speak my schoolgirl French again. It also works out how to do the things I've always wanted to do – I download an app to learn Norwegian, I write my five-year life plan and I stop watching trashy TV.

I write lists and lists of the things I want to achieve, from "find Jacky Rigby" to "go to every museum in Sydney", and from "gold-plate a Shreddie" to "learn taekwondo". I plan research into internet trolls to find out why some people are so vicious online – if I can find out why, I might be able to stop it. I want to find out who the last person to speak Latin as a proper language was, and do a PhD on why it died out. I start planning a possible trip to Paris with Jo when Kai and I are next in Europe. Since her illness I have never been away with her, not even for one night, but now everything seems possible.

But as the weeks wear on, the highs become higher – terrifying me and Kai so much so that I write on one of my lists:

"Check with Dr W. Am I manic?" (Dr John Walker is the psychologist I saw when I had my headaches.)

And lows start appearing, with periods of extreme irritability and anxiety. It's much more of a burden to Kai than to me, as I criticise him and accuse him of not supporting me properly. He deals with it as best he can, just assuming that it's a normal part of me adjusting to motherhood.

During my highs, I have fast and furious conversations with Kai about Life, the Universe and Everything (the Douglas Adams book as well as the concept). Later, he said it was like being back in college, when all things felt possible – within the reach of an outstretched arm and an open mind.

We go to a friend's wedding at Long Reef Golf Club when I'm having one of my highs. In between courses of lovely food, I regale the table with stories, smiling and laughing and bestowing my sparkling wonderfulness to all and sundry.

I am totally over the top, overloud, and overbearing. I catch a few glances between some of the other guests on our table, but don't let that halt the flow of scintillating commentary I believe I am supplying.

I manage to embarrass one of the other guests, a man with red hair and a sharp wit. I've been chatting to the man next to him about his wife, who is Chinese, and can't get a visa to come and live in Australia. Red joins in the conversation and I ask loudly, 'So where is your lovely wife?' He then has to announce to the table that they are separated. There is a tumbleweed moment after that, but one of the other guests manages to start the conversation again. Undaunted, a few minutes later I manage to demolish his argument as to why you shouldn't wash your hands after you've gone to the toilet.

'But they say you've got more germs under your fingernails than under the seat of the average toilet. So, you should really wash the toilet seat after you've touched it with your dirty hands,' he says.

'That's why you shouldn't wash your hands? Because they are too dirty? Really? It's all the more reason to wash your hands!' I reply with a flourish, beaming to all the others on our table. *That'll stump him*, I think.

He pinches his lips together with forefinger and thumb, hiding a thwarted smile.

'Yes, that does make sense,' he says quietly while the rest of the table burst out laughing. He then avoids talking to me for the rest of the meal and between the speeches. We leave just after the dancing starts to get the baby into his bed.

But then the lows come, and I snap at Kai, demanding his help with unimportant tasks, like learning how to use Pinterest, when he's exhausted from disturbed nights and trying to keep up with my racing thoughts.

And my son ... Despite having huge problems with breastfeeding, I am loving being a new mum, and I feel full to the brim with a brand-new type of love. I like learning new things, and now that I've been let in to the wonderful new world of motherhood, I feel like I have the opportunity to learn 20 impossible things before breakfast. Nothing is too much for my little boy.

The times when I am most anxious usually revolve around going out. I worry excessively about the nappy bag: Have I got everything I need? Will I get caught out? My anxiety isn't helped by the fact that nearly every time I go out, I forget some small item that I discover I really need. Having a small baby also makes me worry that I'm constantly going to be late. So I pack and check and recheck the nappy bag, so that I'm ready to go at least 30 minutes early. I worry about the pushchair we have bought, which isn't one of the ones that lies flat. All my other baby-group friends have got flat ones, and I'm convinced that I'm damaging my son's developing spine by putting him in our buggy. Going to my newly established mothers' group is very stressful, though I love the women I meet and am convinced we're all going to become lifelong friends.

As long as I am safe in the flat with my pumping machine, jars of snacks, cups of tea, and my iPad, I'm like the happiest pig in the stinkiest mud. I love it so much that I don't want Kai to miss out, and suggest he take a year's sabbatical after my maternity leave so he can have as much fun and fulfilment as I am having. I'll take care of the bacon-bringing-home business.

As the weeks tick by, I am so excited and brim-full of fantastic thoughts and ideas that I start sleeping less and less. When I do sleep, I have strange, half-wakeful dreams. Kai wakes one early morning to find me tickling him under the chin. When he asks if I'm alright I say, 'I thought you were the baby. There is something about ... something about the woman having to check on the baby more.'

I have always been prone to this semi-sleep talk. One night when we first moved to Australia, I had had an early night. Kai came in to give me a kiss good night, but I was already half asleep. He knelt down to kiss me, and I pushed him away.

'You are like an umbrella,' I snapped. (He had a prickly three-day-old beard.) Then, in my dazed state, realising that wasn't a very good reaction to a lovely bedtime kiss, I gave him some constructive advice: 'Next time, kiss me with the soft of your bottom.'

One night, I wake up four times to jump out of bed in a panic and race to my son's bassinet. I only have a vague memory of this, but Kai tells me that, on one occasion, I jump out of bed and take the duvet with me, waking him up. Another time, Kai wakes up with the baby's cries, only to find me sitting up in bed with my eyes closed.

I say ponderously, 'I seem to be having some difficulty opening my eyes.'

*

My ups are becoming frantic, and I have too many racing thoughts to manage. The scribbles in my journal become less and less easy to understand. I scrawl diagrams on the cover with arrows linking different words and spend hours surfing the net, like people used to do in the 90s – just aimlessly moving from one webpage to another, following any link that takes my fancy. Facebook becomes my site of choice as I try to track down long-lost friends.

I see a picture of a friend called Liz on Facebook and am convinced it will go viral. (This is when Coke are making bottles with names on.) Liz has found a bottle with "Liz" on, and another with "Herrinton". She took a photo of them next to each other and posted it on Facebook. At least, that is what I think the photo shows. I link the photo to one of my friends in London, Will. He has never met or even heard of Liz, but I am convinced if he sees the photo, he will forward it on to his friends and it will go viral. (God knows what Liz thought I was doing, or Will for that matter.)

Later, one of my friends back in the UK, who had a baby a month before me, but has been having a more normal experience of how hard it is having a young baby, says she can't quite believe how "perky" I am in my Facebook updates. One of these updates says, "Things I didn't expect about being a mum – more time to write, not less." I don't add that this is because my sleep hours are dwindling from five hours to four, then to three.

*

I express milk for a week after I leave the hospital until my nipples recover enough to start breastfeeding again. I'm a bit addicted to the *ammetåke* feeling from the breast pump and am happy to discover that, after the first toe-curling painful seconds, the same chilled-out, bliss feelings settle over me when I'm breastfeeding. I love the sight of my dark-haired boy snuggling at my breast, drinking his fill.

But, as it is still painful, I go to see one of the staff at the Early Childhood Health Care Clinic in Manly and get her to watch my latch. She gives me the thumbs-up, but is worried I might have thrush on my nipples. She thinks this might be why they've been hurting. Thrush is caused by a fungus that occurs naturally in the body. It's usually kept under control by "friendly" bacteria, but it can occur in the baby's mouth and then be passed onto the mum's nipples while breastfeeding.

I also show her my less than gentle method for getting him off the breast and she says, 'Whatever works for you, darl.'

'I'm sort of getting used to the pain,' I say. But, after seeing how easy other mothers are finding breastfeeding, I realise something is still not going well for us.

'It really shouldn't hurt that much,' she agrees, confirming my thoughts.

The pain gets worse and worse, and in week five I go back to expressing. You need to keep stimulating the breast to make sure your milk supply doesn't dry up. I am up twice a night to express then feed and, despite Kai loyally getting up to help, it all adds to my sleeplessness. And, of course, once I'm up, I just have to check Facebook, as it's the middle of the day in the UK. It makes perfect sense to me.

People ask me how the baby is sleeping, and I say, 'Fine', because he is a brilliant sleeper. But no one asks me how I am sleeping. And therein lies the rub.

CHAPTER 9

DON'T YOU KNOW I'M LOCO?

Dr Martin Luther King said, 'I have a dream', and then he woke up.

My diary entry.

The psychosis starts with Renée Zellweger.

Before the baby's arrival, I had a chat with one of our neighbours. Emily is a lovely lady in her sixties with a silver bob and bright eyes. She's from England and swims in the sea every day no matter what the weather. As we chatted, both folding our respective washing from the line, she told me that her daughter – whose child was due around the same time as ours – is coming over from LA to stay with her.

'How wonderful,' I said.

'She's an actor.'

'Really cool.'

This fact lodged itself deep in my brain.

It is now Monday of week six, and as we are leaving the apartment, I see a woman clutching a very small baby. *Ah*, I think, *that must be Emily's daughter*. Her face looks very familiar.

That morning we have the six-week check for mother and baby with Dr Harper. Kai is going in to work late so he can come with me. While waiting in the reception I flick through a copy of Grazia and see a photo of a woman clutching a small baby. It looks exactly like Emily's daughter. I check the name by the picture. Renée Zellweger.

It isn't a very flattering shot; she's wearing thick-rimmed glasses and her already-small eyes are squinted into raisins in her round pale face. It is also quite blurry like it was shot from a distance and the photo editor had magnified it many times.

'Oh, my God,' I say to Kai. 'I think Renée Zellweger is in our building. She's Emily's daughter.'

'I don't think so, Jen,' says Kai. 'Are you feeling okay?'

'Yes, sure – I'm just so happy.'

I carry on flicking through the magazine and hit on another photo which stops me in my tracks.

'Look – it's Howard!'

I wave the magazine at Kai. The photo shows the new mystery man in Sandra Bullock's life. He looks exactly like a crazy party-hound called Howard, an old college friend of Kai's.

'That isn't Howard.'

'Yes, it is.'

'It isn't, Jen. I know Howard and that isn't him.'

'But it looks exactly like him – and he knows famous people, doesn't he?'

'He does, yes. But that's not him.'

He turns back to his iPhone to check his work emails. I know it's Howard; Kai just isn't looking properly. *He works too hard.* I turn the page of the magazine and see a photo of Halle Berry – but wait, that looks just like my friend Gina! I stare at the photo. I haven't seen Gina in a while; maybe she's secretly living a double life in Tufnell Park when she's not in LA ... Then I see a picture of Lindsay Lohan and it is our friend Clare, who's married to Kai's old uni friend, Peter.

The magazine is transformed from a glossy gossip mag into an item of extreme importance. It seems to glow with secret knowledge in my hands. I turn the next page as though I'm in the British Library handling Shakespeare's *First Folio* with white-gloved hands. *How do I know all these famous people? This seems so odd.* Then a thought occurs to me. *Maybe I'm famous too.*

I look around the waiting room and feel a great upwelling of happiness. I am beaming. I catch the eye of a mother, sitting opposite me with her child. She gives me a brief smile then looks away, embarrassed. I notice one of the receptionists glancing at me, too.

Why is everyone acting so weirdly towards me? I wonder. I turn another page of the magazine and see a picture of Cameron Diaz. And she looks exactly like me.

Oh, my God, I'm Cameron Diaz.

I look at Kai and he smiles back at me. In the picture, Cameron is wearing the blue shirt and cut-off shorts that I wear all the time. *I must have come to Australia, like Renée, to get away from the paparazzi while we have our baby.*

I look at Kai again and think, *the lucky bastard, he gets to have sex with Cameron Diaz / Me.*

I am tallish, and was slim before the baby came. I like surfing. I have blonde hair and I love dancing. These things prove I must be Cameron Diaz. (My addled brain is conveniently ignoring the things we don't have in common, like me not being a world-famous movie star who once went out with Justin Timberlake.)

You may think this doesn't make sense – surely I must know I'm not Cameron Diaz? But I don't and here's why. I think I'm Cameron Diaz, which is quite a mad thing to think, so I'm either mad or I'm Cameron Diaz. I know I'm not mad; I survived the horrendous night in the hospital. Therefore, I *must* be Cameron Diaz. You see? At the time, it seemed like a simple mathematical equation.

'The doctor is ready for you now,' says the receptionist, and I carefully put the precious magazine down. I am blazing with happiness and a bit wobbly on my feet, as you might expect you would be after discovering you're a world-famous actress who has secretly moved to Australia to have a baby with her "civilian" husband.

'How are you doing, Jen?' asks the doctor.

I flash him a knowing smile. *So, we're all just going to go along with my alias. That's fine by me.*

'Well, my scar is still weeping a bit and sore in parts, but other than that I'm fine. I'm really happy actually.'

He smiles at me and Kai.

'Let me take a look.'

I hop up onto the couch, lift my dress and roll down the top of my knickers.

'How is the little one?' he asks as he bends over my nether regions.

'He is a little angel, really – the perfect baby.'

My son gurgles in the buggy as if in agreement.

Dr Harper looks at me and raises his eyebrows. I imagine new mums aren't usually filled with such unbridled enthusiasm at week six. But then, not many new mums have come to the startling realisation that they are one of the most beautiful women in the world.

'Good. Then let's have a look here.' Dr Harper pauses and frowns, bending further over me to get a closer look. 'I think I know why your scar isn't healing properly. They've left part of the stitch material in.'

'Oh,' I say, a million miles away thinking about my jet-set lifestyle in Hollywood, and what I'm going to do next in my career.

'I'm really sorry about this, Jen. I'll be having stern words with the hospital.'

'That's okay; everyone makes mistakes sometimes.'

'You'll need to take a course of antibiotics.'

'No problems.'

He reaches for some metal pincers and sets about pulling out what looks like a very manky piece of blue string. It breaks open two of the scabs, which start to bleed again. He presses a pad of white cotton-wool dressing to the wound.

'There, that should do it, Jen.'

He helps me to my feet and I rearrange my dress. *Should I just say it? We are safe here in his little office; no one is going to know if I just come out with it …*

I laugh and give him a wink. 'I can't thank you enough for everything you've done. I'm so happy!'

My famous megawatt smile almost blinds him. I bet it's pretty unnerving having such a famous patient.

We are clustered at the door of his office in an awkward bundle. He reaches his hand out, but I go for his cheek instead and he laughs. I imagine him telling his wife, 'Cameron Diaz kissed me today', and them both laughing over it.

'You do seem very happy,' he agrees as he shakes Kai's hand.

As we head down in the lift, I give Kai a massive hug. I can see us reflected in the polished metal of the lift wall and I stare in disbelief. I don't see Cameron Diaz's face staring back at me. It is just plain old Jen.

'I'm not Cameron Diaz, am I?' I ask.

Kai pulls out of the hug and looks me hard in the face.

'Are you sure you're okay?'

I laugh. 'Yeah.'

He frowns at me and I smile back at him.

'What do you mean then?'

'Oh nothing,' I say. 'Just a thought.'

CHAPTER 10

I'M JUST A VOICE INSIDE YOUR HEAD. I CAN'T HELP YOU. HELP YOURSELF.

What are delusions, really, but just thoughts from an over-active brain? The way I've always understood my sister's illness is that she has too much dopamine in one part of her brain. Dopamine is one of a few neurotransmitters that help electrical impulses leap across the gap between brain cells. Having too much means that your brain makes too many leaps, and you start believing – as my sister did – that you can fly, communicate telepathically, or hear what the neighbours are really saying about you behind your back. Your brain literally jumps to conclusions.

Of course, the reality of schizophrenia is much more complex than just an overabundance of dopamine. If it was as simple as that, then we would have cured it by now. Scientists are still puzzling out this complex and devastating illness.

I once asked my sister about the voices she hears when her brain is misfiring.

'If you know they aren't real, can't you just ignore them?' I asked.

'Okay, let's do an experiment,' she said.

'Okay.'

'Talk to me. Just say anything you like.'

'Um ... well, it is lovely to see–'

'You're *shit*!' she hissed into my ear.

'What?'

'Go on, just ignore it.'

'Oh.'

'Go on. Try again.'

I was silent for a second. Her face was intent. *She really wants me to understand this*. So I tried again.

'I'm having a great–'

She moved to stand behind me and whispered into my ear, 'I'm behind you.' Her voice was quiet, filled with menace. 'Don't turn around or I'll–'

'Stop. Stop, please,' I pleaded. My heart had grown cold. 'I think I get it. Is it really that bad?'

'Yes. Sometimes worse.'

'That's horrible, Jo.'

I looked at her and she smiled back at me. Her look took me back to our childhood – it was the look an older sister gives a younger one when she is explaining something important and complicated. Love flooded through me at the reminder of how close we were. The old us resurfaced, reconnected, and faded. Then we were back at the busy junction at Manor House station, standing outside the bagel shop with 253s and 29s roaring past us towards Finsbury Park, and the noises bouncing off the cold grey pavements and tarmac around us. The horror returned.

'That's what it's like. They sound as real as your voice does to me now.'

The glimpse into her mind filled me with horror at what she had to endure and a new feeling of amazement at, given the circumstances, how well she coped. 'How do you cope with it?'

She smiled and shrugged, and we carried on with our walk into Finsbury Park, away from the noise and the grey and into the green of the grass and trees.

CHAPTER 11

I'LL SEE YOU ON THE DARK SIDE OF THE MOON

The next day is Tuesday, and mothers' group looms.

Kai works from home on a Tuesday. I am having one of my downs, begging him to drive me to mothers' group.

'I can't do it on my own. You just have no idea how hard it is for me to drive with a baby in the car.'

Most people are completely blind to how risky driving a car is. For people who don't smoke, it's usually the riskiest thing they will do in a day. I have always prided myself on my "actual risk, as opposed to perceived risk" mindset being grounded in fact and rationality, and I use it to make sure I reduce risk by not speeding, not tailgating, not drinking and driving, etc. But now, with my son in the car, this risk balloons up in my chest and rises in a bubble of pressure around my head, making it impossible to consider putting him in the car seat and speeding through Sydney traffic. Strangely it doesn't affect me if Kai is driving, only if the responsibility is mine.

'Don't worry, Jen, I'll drive you. It's only up the road.'

'It may only be up the road to you, but it isn't for me. I have no idea if I'll find parking. It's ... it's ...'

'I said I'll take you, Jen.'

'Okay, okay. Thanks,' I mutter, looking around the room. I try to calm myself down, but the fear grabs me again. 'I mean, I've no idea what I am supposed to pack to take with me.'

'Just what we normally pack: nappies, bottles and–'

'Oh, it's all so easy for you, isn't it? I can't do it. I *can't*. Please help me!'

I dissolve into tears, overwhelmed by the enormity of what I am supposed to be able to do and my complete lack of faith in my ability to do it. Making everything worse is the faint echo of the knowledge that I am, like everyone always says about me, overreacting. (One of my nicknames when I was a child was "Cry-Baby Onion". We were all assigned vegetables and I guess I got onion because they make you cry. My sister was Lanky Leek, because she was taller than the rest of us. Hardly surprising given she was older than most of us. My friend was Pea-Head Penny as she had a small head (she doesn't really). Children, eh? This narrative has followed me around ever since, but I have come to realise as I've got older that I am simply sensitive, not over-sensitive.

This is an easy, everyday task, a little whisper says in my ear. *What is wrong with me?*

Kai gets up from his desk and comes over and takes my hand.

'You don't have to go if you don't want to.'

'But I have to get used to leaving the flat with the baby. Otherwise it'll be terrible.'

'What will?'

'Everything.'

He calmly helps me pack up the nappy bag and makes sure I have everything: my phone, my wallet and keys.

'See, you'll be okay.'

I grip my hands together as he shoulders the bag and gives me a tired smile. There is a hard lump in my throat and a feeling like hunger in my stomach though I've just eaten. 'I'm so sorry, babes, I don't know what's wrong with me today. I feel so wired and anxious.'

We drive the short distance to the Early Childhood Health Care Clinic where the mothers' group is being held. (In Australia, the government brings together groups of women who have had babies within a few weeks of each other and facilitates three or four weekly groups until friendships form.) Kai drops me off and I take a deep breath and walk into the room.

I smile as I see Rosie, one of the friendly women in the group, and the anxiety starts to ebb. *I can do this. I can do this.* I sit down and Kath, the Early Childhood Nurse, smiles her hello. The room fills up and Kath starts her talk on settling techniques.

The room is rapt, listening intently.

'What do we do if they just keep waking up?' someone asks.

I laugh.

'Well, you just have to keep trying,' Kath says.

I laugh again. Kath glances at me with a concerned expression. The other mums seem absorbed in their own little ones, adjusting dribble bibs and patting soft, warm backs.

'What do you do if you have the best baby in the world?' I ask.

Now everyone laughs. I pick up my son and hold him up. Everyone is looking at me. I am controlling the room – if I laugh, I can make them laugh too.

Kath starts talking again and the hour goes by in a blur. I'd booked Kath to check The Boy, so I grab her at the end as all the others file out.

Kath and I go into her office. It overlooks the car park, where I can see Kai pacing up and down on the phone. Her office has a large, L-shaped desk piled with papers, and a counter along one of the walls with scales and nappy-changing equipment.

'Pop him up here on the scales.'

She watches the display and jots down notes in our "Blue Book". This is a folder given to each new mum to keep track of their baby's growth, development, and any medical issues. (In the UK, mums are issued with a "Red Book".)

'He is a good weight,' she states as he wiggles and squirms. 'Yes, he is a healthy, thriving boy.'

'Thank you, thank you,' I say, and let out a huge breath I didn't even realise I was holding. *He's okay,* I say to myself. *Everything is okay. He has passed the six-week test!*

When I go to leave, she puts her hand on my arm.

'And how are you?' she asks gently.

'I'm really good; not sleeping much but that's par for the course, isn't it?'

'Yes, it is I'm afraid. Are you having difficulty settling him?'

'No, he sleeps really well. It's me having trouble getting to sleep.'

'Really? Why?'

'I'm too excited, I guess. I love being a mum so much. I love it, love it, love it!' I feel a bubble of uncontrollable laughter rise up from my stomach and I let it out in a rush as I gaze down at my son. I can feel a smile stretching my face wide.

But when I look up at Kath, she is silent.

I go to pick up the baby and wave at Kai through the window.

'Wait for a minute,' says Kath. 'Is that your partner?'

'Yes. He is half Norwegian. We got married last year. It was wonderful, really such a wonderful day!' My words are coming tumbling out over one another.

I wave at Kai to come in. After a few moments he knocks lightly on the door and comes into the room.

'The baby is all good! He passed! He passed!' I tell him. I can feel the laughter threatening to overwhelm me again, but it's just such good news!

'Ah okay, that's good I guess–'

'And this is Kath,' I interrupt.

'I have a book I want to recommend to you,' she says riffling through the papers on her desk, but I brush her off.

'We should get going.'

'Just one more minute,' Kath insists. 'Where did you work before bubs?'

'At the Cerebral Palsy Alliance,' I say. 'They are such a great organisation. Have you heard of them?'

'Yes, they're marvellous.'

Kath won't stop asking me questions, and she's starting to get on my nerves. I just want to leave! I look at Kai, but he is waiting patiently as ever for Kath to stop fussing and flapping. I can feel the anxiety radiating out of her. *But she said the baby is fine, why should she be worried?* The wave of anxiety reaches out from her to me and I take a step backwards. *I need to get away from her.*

'I'm going to wait in the car,' I declare. I pick the baby up and grab the car keys from Kai, before rushing from the room. 'You get the bag, babe?' I call behind me, but I catch Kath holding up a hand to my husband.

Ignoring it, I run to the car and focus all my attention on getting my son into his seat.

Kai and Kath are taking ages. I can see them chatting through the window, and grimace at him when Kath is looking down at something on her desk.

'Come on,' I mouth. Kai doesn't notice. I think about knocking on the glass, but something about the way their heads are leaning closely together stops me.

What I didn't know was that Kath was stalling while she found the number of the Extended Hours Team – previously known as the Mental Health Crisis Team. There's a good name change, if ever I heard one!

She had started getting alarmed during the mothers' group. She told him about my odd behaviour – laughing when there was no need to, and claiming I had the best baby in the world.

'Is she always like this?' she asks Kai.

'No, she's very much not like this. She's not getting much sleep.'

'I think something more serious is happening and I'd like you to ring the Extended Hours Team.' She hands over a yellow Post-it note with a number scrawled on it.

When we get back to our apartment, Kai suggests I have a nap while he looks after the baby. I plunge gratefully into bed and fall into a fitful sleep.

An hour and a half later, he comes to wake me up. Sitting on the edge of the bed, he says,

'Jen, some people are coming around. We are all very worried about you and think you might need some help.'

My heart leaps, and I'm gripped by fear.

'"People"? What do you mean?'

After all these years, it was finally happening. I imagine the people, serious doctors and nurses looking down on me, standing around me as I sit up in bed. They are pointing at me.

Unbalanced, unbalanced, unbalanced.

'They are from the Extended Hours Team.'

Even though they've changed the name, I still know what it means. I inch back in the bed, away from his calming hands.

'No. No. No!'

'It's going to be alright, Jen.'

Kai is looking at me with soft, sad eyes and he sounds so miserable, so tired.

'No, it isn't. I'm going mad, aren't I? They're going to section me, aren't they?!'

'I won't let that happen.'

'You won't be able to do anything about it. This is really it, isn't it? I'm going mad.'

I start to cry desperate tears and try to get out of bed, but Kai stops me.

'Jen, everything is going to be fine. They are here to help. I've explained at great length about Jo and your fear of going mad.'

He holds me tight as the tears spill and spill.

We hear a knock on the door.

'I'm going to get that, okay?'

He leaves the room, and I sit in bed with the madness harrying me like a terrier, nipping and pulling. I grip the duvet tight and take a deep breath. I think about the help button in the hospital. Now my time really has come.

CHAPTER 12

JUST ME, MYSELF AND I

I come out of the bedroom into the sitting room. There are two strange people there, one sitting on our brown leather rocking chair and the other on the brown textured ottoman.

They both smile at me.

'Hi, Jen, I'm Mark from the Extended Hours Team,' says one. He is a stocky man with a barrel-like chest and a brown smiling face. He has a black briefcase like my mother used to have back in the 80s.

'I'm Claudette,' says the other. She is English with dark straight hair and a flick of eyeliner at the corner of each eye.

These two people sit in my home and look at me. I start crying again, and Kai comes over to me.

'It's alright, Jen; they're just here to help.'

'That's right,' confirms Mark. 'Can you tell us what's been going on?'

I sit still for a moment on the sofa next to Kai.

'I think I'm losing my mind,' I admit.

I tell them about my fear of going mad like my sister and that we are approaching 15th March – the anniversary of her first breakdown.

'That sounds very tough, Jen. But what you are going through is nothing like schizophrenia.'

The relief washes over me and I feel my whole body relax. 'Really? Are you sure?'

'Yes, absolutely.'

'What is it then?'

'We think it is caused by extreme sleeplessness.'

'Okay, that makes sense.'

'We will give you some medication to help you fall asleep, and recommend you give up breastfeeding so you can get good, long stretches of sleep. Your husband can give your son a bottle.'

'But I don't want to give up breastfeeding! I want to give my child the best. Everyone says, "breast is best".'

Why would I have to sign a release form in hospital to get bottled milk if it wasn't bad? I don't want to give up on breastfeeding! I've tried so hard!

They ask me some questions about how I'm feeling within myself, towards my son.

'I know this is hard to hear but have you had any thoughts of harming yourself?'

'No.'

'Or harming anyone else? Your son?'

'God, no.'

I look over at Kai, but he's looking down at his hands. *Surely, they all know I would never, never hurt my baby?* Little did I know that I would have to get used to being asked this question.

They are calm, gentle, and kind. They aren't going to make me do anything I don't want to do, I realise. I talk about thinking I was Cameron Diaz and they laugh along with me.

'It is a very strange feeling,' I say.

'You probably should stop reading those gossip mags!' jokes Mark.

Eventually, after what feels like hours of talking back and forth, they prescribe temazepam, a sedative used to treat insomnia.

'We recommend that you stop breastfeeding while you catch up on sleep, and while taking these drugs,' Claudette informs me.

'So I should just express milk until I stop taking the medication and can go back to breastfeeding?'

'We don't know how long it will take.'

'I don't want to stop breastfeeding,' I say again. 'I need to carry on.'

'Jen, it is more important for your son to have a well mother than breastmilk.'

Even though I don't think there is anything wrong with bottle-feeding, I am consumed with sadness at the idea of having to forgo breastfeeding. Society places such a high premium on it. Women are put under enormous pressure, because yes, it is better for the baby, and let's not forget cheaper, too. It simply hadn't occurred to me that I wouldn't be able to do this for my own son. During our antenatal classes, the women had said, 'For every problem a mum has with breastfeeding, there is always an answer.' *Well, not for this one*, I thought.

They also want me to stop taking the amitriptyline as it is a mood elevator and my mood is already quite elevated. They say they will keep monitoring me.

'You should be fine once you've caught up on sleep.'

Mark flips open the black briefcase and hands over one pill. I hold it in the palm of my hand. One small tablet that I must take. I look up at Mark again and he smiles reassuringly back at me.

'My sister used to be very resistant about taking her meds,' I say, and gulp down the pill. I want to show them how different I am, how I've learnt from her mistakes.

'What you have is nothing like your sister's illness, you have to remember that,' says Claudette. They're both smiling still.

There's an awkward silence. It feels like they will never leave.

'Well, thanks for coming over,' I say, sounding like a proud host at the end of a particularly successful dinner party rather than a woman saying goodbye to a mental health crisis team. Kai gives me a wonky look, eyebrows raised.

As we finally shut the door behind them Kai pulls me into a big hug.

'See, that was okay!'

'I thought they'd never go.'

'You are going to be okay – do you believe that now?'

I shrug. I don't believe that at all.

(What I don't know is that, after their visit, they ring Kai and tell him I could be a risk to my son and to myself. They tell him not to leave me on my own with him, or on my own, full stop.)

*

Over the next week, we are visited by two people, twice a day. Kai has to take the week off work. Twice a day we sit on the sofa and everyone looks at me as I tell them what I am going through. They ask questions and I answer to the best of my ability. I meet three Mathews, Claudette, Sandra, Jane, Tianna, and Mark.

During each visit, time drags. Despite their kindness and professional concern, I feel their scrutiny like ants on my skin. I am convinced that they won't go unless Kai or I actually ask them to. I feel that I can't ask them as they might start wondering what I have to hide, so we work out a system: when I go to the bathroom, Kai knows this is my signal for him to wrap up the conversation.

At first, they say that what I am experiencing is caused by sensitivity to the incredible hormone soup racing around my body, as well as a severe lack of sleep. And indeed, for the first two days, things seem to calm down once I get a couple of decent nights' rest.

'You must protect your sleep,' they tell me. 'That is really important.'

But by the end of the week, despite the meds and the restorative sleep, we all agree things are getting worse. I'm having more and more strange thoughts, along with periods of elation followed by crushing anxiety, and they start talking about postpartum psychosis (PPP). This term covers a collection of mental illnesses that occur once or twice in every thousand births. Those with postpartum psychosis often have delusional beliefs and hallucinations, but many make a full recovery within months.

The team try me on a new drug: an antipsychotic called olanzapine, prescribed for my mania and delusions. It was developed as a treatment for schizophrenia and bipolar disorder, but it can also be used as a mood stabiliser and for the general treatment of psychosis. It is the same drug that Jo used to take when she was first ill.

This isn't helping my fear of going mad like my sister. This is a Big Deal. A Very Big Deal. I feel that, by taking olanzapine, I am taking a step closer to schizophrenia, to being just as ill as Jo, to a wretched life of pain, confusion, and paranoia. I feel frightened and hopeless, even though I know I need to take the medication to get better.

In theory, I should get a full night's sleep with Kai feeding my son expressed milk, topped up with formula. But I can't give up the idea of returning to breastfeeding, and so I am still pumping. I wake up when Kai creeps back into bed. He tells me later that he would sit in the bedroom listening to me move around the flat, bone tired but fearful of what I might do. Sometimes he would get up and find me in my son's room with the lights blazing, staring down at our boy. Sometimes I would pick The Boy up, usually just after Kai had spent hours trying to settle him. Once, I just stood in front of the fridge until Kai gently led me back to bed. Another time, I shut my son's bedroom door in Kai's face and wouldn't let him in.

Other nights I stay up watching episodes of *Thirty Rock* over and over again. I become convinced that, since my brain is working at such a high level now, I'm somehow seeing each individual frame of film. I "see" so fast that I can see frames of film that the editor hadn't cut quite enough. I replay the same episode over and over, "seeing" more and more of these "out-takes". Once, I think I see an unscripted interaction between Tina Fey and the other actors that is funnier than the rest (which is already pretty effing hilarious). I think that Kenneth is my friend Chris, and that I went to school with Dot Com.

I also watch YouTube videos of De La Soul songs over and over. I become convinced that my first boyfriend at school was Plug One and that all De La Soul songs are messages to me from him. I get particularly hooked on 'Three is a Magic Number' – it's very significant; three must really be the magic number because of what happened to me at the maternity hospital (I thought that my manic crying session had happened on the third day of my son's life rather than the sixth. Nevertheless, it doesn't faze me when I check my diary and find out that it was, in fact, Day Six. After all, six is just twice three, so it is doubly the magic number!).

I know now that when you are having delusions you will twist all things around to make your delusion right. The conviction that the delusion is real is so strong that reality warps around it like light around a black hole. It has made me much more understanding of my sister when she clings to what I think are delusions, but she thinks are real.

Not all my delusions and manic thoughts were unpleasant; in fact, some of the time I felt euphoric. However, this period was by far the hardest time for Kai, being so worried in case the psychiatric nurses were right and I was a danger to my son or myself. He took them at their word and never left me alone with my son, but couldn't always look after me at the same time. I can't imagine how awful this period was for Kai. When he first told me about it, I was wracked with guilt and sorrow at the pain I caused him.

Some women with postpartum psychosis hear voices telling them to hurt their child or themselves. I'm lucky, in the midst of such overarching bad luck, that this didn't happen to me.

CHAPTER 13

LIGHT MY CANDLES IN A DAZE

It is the middle of the night. Kai is feeding my son as I'm pumping (I still can't give up the hope that I'll be able to go back to breastfeeding when all this is over). When I slip back into bed, the two of us lie there awake. He's trying to wait for me to fall asleep, but the exhaustion of the last few days catches up with him and he slips under first.

I, as tired as I am, lie awake listening to his breathing.

The walls and ceiling are moving, bending. I breathe in and the walls bend towards me, breathe out and they shimmer back into place. I know I'm not mad, but if I'm sane then the walls really are moving. *What if the walls are appearing to move for some other unknown reason?* But what could it be? I breathe in and the room contracts again, breathe out and it expands.

Silently, I get up and close the door behind me as Kai rolls over in his sleep. I go and check on my son. He is flat on his back, sparked out. I watch him sleep, his breath rasping quietly like a velvet cricket. The room blurs and shimmers in the dark.

I go into the bathroom and splash my face with water. It is 2.30am. I hear a thump against the bathroom door and spin around quickly, but it's nothing. I lean over the sink. *Get a grip, Jen. Get a grip.*

The pink and blue square tiles on the floor start jumping and moving. Shapes fall like Tetris. I grip the edge of the sink and the room swirls around me.

When I slowly lift my gaze to the mirror, I see someone else's face. She looks like me but with a smaller button nose, and she has grey eyes where my blue ones should be. There is a stripe of red down the side of her face. It is throbbing. I lift my hand, and she lifts hers, too, both of us feeling the tenderness around the red, raised bump.

I turn around and look at the white painted bathroom door. It is blurring and changing colour as I hear another thump.

The door is now scrubbed pine.

It is 1962.

He is just outside. I know that. I start to pant, leaning on the sink.

The handle turns slowly.

'Annie,' he calls in a rough whisper.

'Annie, no need to hide. I'll be gentle with you.'

The handle turns again and he rattles the door.

'Undo the lock, Annie. Come on, girl. We both know this is going to happen; I've seen the way you look at me.'

They'd both been smashed drunk when they came in a few hours earlier; my husband, Tom, and his friend Jack. Friday meant only one thing for them: payday and the pub. I'd tried to serve them up the stew I'd made but they both laughed and slapped the table.

'Eating is cheating,' Jack had said.

'We're thirsty not hungry,' Tom laughed. He'd opened up a bottle of whisky and placed it on the table between

the plates of rapidly cooling stew. They'd drunk and drunk, their talk getting louder and louder. It was all about the boss they called Captain and all the ways he was a failure: a nit-picking, penny-pinching, no-good weakling.

I leave them to it and start on the washing up. I hear their raucous voices getting louder and louder as I rinse the plates in the soapy water. Then I notice it has fallen quiet, and I realise, with a jolt, that Jack is leaning in the kitchen doorway.

'You know, you are a fine-looking woman, Annie,' he says.

'Jack, that's the drink—'

Then he lunges at me, catching me with his open hand around the side of my face. But in his drunkenness, he misjudges the distance and crashes into the side of the sink. In a flash I twist away from him and run to the bathroom, slamming the door and turning the key just as he comes stumbling after me.

'You bitch, let me in!' he demands, and starts banging the door in earnest. The lock is holding, for now.

And where is Tom in all this? Probably passed out, drunk in his chair.

Jack bangs again and the wood around the lock starts to splinter.

'Tom!' I scream. 'Tom, where are you? Tom! Tom!'

With each cry, Jack attacks the door with renewed vigour, kicking at the lock. The wood splinters further and further each time.

'I'm almost in,' Jack threatens in between heavy breaths.

Then I hear an almighty roar.

'Jack!'

And then a heavy thud and slide.

'Get out — get out!' Tom yells.

'She led me on, Tom. You know what she's like.'

'Get. Out. Now!'

I hear the front door open and bang shut.

'Annie, it's me,' Tom says. 'You're okay now.'

'Am I?' I shout at him. 'Where were you? How could you bring this into our home?'

'He's gone now, Annie. It's safe to come out.'

I lean my head against the door.

'Is he gone?'

I reach down for the lock. The key has gone, a simple slide lock in its place. I crease my brows.

'Tom?' I call... to silence.

The door is changing back to the thick white paint, the pine gone. I slide open the lock carefully, but all that is waiting for me is the kitchen – familiar, dark, and empty. I touch my face to find that the swelling has disappeared. I am back in the now.

I cross the room and sit on the rocking chair, staring out of the window into the dark night. My hands rest loosely together in my lap. Our apartment is high up over the Manly to Spit Bridge scenic walk, and in the day, we have views over to The Heads and across to Forty Baskets beach. The Heads are two rocky headlands, one north, one south, that flank the entrance to Sydney Harbour. Now, though, all is dark, apart from the green light on a marker buoy, which flashes on, flashes off.

I am calm again. I know that I can deal with whatever is coming. Taking a deep breath, I release it in a big sigh and rock backwards and forwards in the chair.

The room around me fades away. The windows and walls softly melt and turn into dark leaves and branches, just like Max's bedroom in *Where the Wild Things Are*.

I am up high in the branches of a paper-bark tree. I reach out and touch the flaky bark with my outstretched hand. My skin is dark brown. I am an Aboriginal woman. It is 1788.

The dark night lightens. The stars and moon fade and a golden twilight illuminates the undersides of the clouds.

I can see the green-cloaked headland of North Heads, fronted by the yellow sand of Spring Cove. The buildings around the beach that make up the Quarantine Station are gone. The gap of open ocean is framed on the other side by the craggy cliffs of South Head. The buildings on South Head are also gone. All around me is pristine bush, with waving branches and twinkling water.

This is the entrance to our territory. The territory of the Guringai people, my people. The sky lightens more until it is the sparkling light of late morning. I see a great canoe coming in through The Heads. It has thick straight poles, the height of trees, decorated by large bright flashes of white cloths. The canoe seems to move without paddles, blown by the winds of the sea. I have never seen anything like it.

'It is so big,' I say to Banjora, who is in the tree next to me.

'Yes,' he agrees. 'The biggest I've ever seen.'

The wind rustles the silver and green leaves, bringing the eucalyptus-scented breath of the ocean.

'We must tell the Elders about this,' he says as we climb backwards down the tree. He gives me a light kiss and we set off at a fast-paced run.

The Elders quickly gather two groups to run in either direction along the waterline to see where this strange canoe is going to land. I go with the first group and Banjora goes with the second. I am speeding along the path that skirts the water's edge, and I can feel the earth slapping against my feet as we race along. We get to a narrow sandy beach on the north side of the water; it is a perfect landing spot, and we wait out of sight in the bush.

The canoe looks even larger now, so, so big. It is big enough to have a smaller, rounder canoe attached to it. We can see men, white men, scrambling all over it. Some are climbing down into the small canoe, which they pull along towards the beach with long, straight paddles. The men are wearing cloth coverings all over their bodies, and the sound of their unfamiliar calls carries over the water.

As they pull the canoe up onto the sand, we step out of the bush. They freeze and then cluster closer together in a tight knot. I can hear the gibberish that is their language as they talk to one another.

'What do you want here?' asks Killara, the eldest in our group.

They shout and laugh. Some of the men point at me and the other women, and one of them moves his hands to his chest, hands curving. A gust of wind blows their smell over to us: grim sweat and rotten fish. Three of them are holding blunt, metal staffs that appear to be their weapons. We have our spears.

One of them steps forward with his hand raised. His face is burnt deep red and his eyes are like two fragments of the sky. He has a hat made of stiff black material and a dark-blue cloak over his body. He makes the motion of a cup tipping into his mouth.

'Waa-ter, waa-ter,' he says.

The other men are collecting together in a tight knot behind him with their metal staffs pointing out towards us. One of the men points at me again and says something that makes all the other men laugh. The leader quiets them with a harsh word.

'You are not welcome here,' says Killara, stepping forward.

One of the metal staffs explodes with a flash and Killara is knocked off his feet, a great gaping hole in his stomach. He screams in pain. Dragging him back, we retreat into the trees, but the men come running after us. One of them grabs my arm and pulls me towards the small canoe, but a great spear flashes past me into *the man's side. I turn and see Banjora as he pulls the spear out of the fallen man's body. He grabs my hand and pulls me away down the track. There are two more thunderclaps from the white men's metal staffs.*

But as I dart back along the path, I realise that I am, in fact, still. I can feel the earth, leaves and twigs beneath my feet, and my back resting on the rocking chair. My chest is heaving from running but at the same time it is calm and measured. In softly and out relaxed. The fright and the pain fade away.

I look around and I'm back in the room.

I must be regressing through my past lives.

This is doubly confusing to me, as deep down I know I don't believe in past lives. *So the Buddhists are right; we do come back to this planet over and over again until we learn what we need to learn.* I sense I'm so close to nirvana, but I don't want to go. The thought of never seeing Kai or my son again if I were to disappear into nirvana fills me with a crushing sadness – but only for a moment. I breathe a sigh of relief when I realise that this unbreakable attachment to the two men in my life means I will stay firmly on the earth.

The room starts to blur and shimmer again. I can feel myself spiralling back though time, like *The Big Bang Theory* credits in reverse. Back, back, back I go. Time whirls around me. Back before Christ was born, before we built the pyramids, before there were roads, back, back, back.

I'm still surrounded by leaves and branches, and the morning sun still shines patchily on the ground. I look down and stroke my forearm. I am covered in dark soft fur, but my palms are pink and hairless. My arms are incredibly strong. I lift my hands to my face and feel the fur on my cheeks and forehead. "Oo oo"-ing my lips into a monkey pout, I look to my left and see another like me standing by my side. We are in a clearing in a dense forest.

I am Eve, the first human, and my mate standing next to me is my Adam. I hold out my hand and he takes it in his, stroking the back with his long fingers. He turns to me and says the first words ever spoken.

'I love you.'

'I love you,' I say back.

Another voice chimes in. 'Jen.'

The trees and earth fade away and the night draws in around me again. I'm back in the sitting room and Kai is rubbing his eyes and coming out of the bedroom.

'What are you doing up?'

'Weird things are happening,' I announce.

He kneels before me and holds my hands. 'What things?'

'I understand so much now,' I say.

'Come to bed. Please, Jen.'

'I know why the caged bird sings.'

'Jen, *please*.'

CHAPTER 14

STOP PLAYING WITH MY DELIRIUM

It is Friday afternoon and Kai and I are arguing again. It seems one of the impacts of my illness is that it makes me hugely argumentative and irritable, shattering our usually harmonious relationship.

'Please, just look at this. It will explain everything.' I thrust my notebook at him.

He looks down at the diagram.

'Well, do you get it now? Do you understand why all arguments are circular?'

He looks up at me sadly and says nothing.

'Well?'

'No, Jen, I don't, but–

'I can't stand it anymore! You must understand it; it's so clear. We've been over and over this – you must get it!'

'I'm sorry, but it just doesn't make sense.'

'It is so obvious. All arguments are circular because they are. That proves it.'

He says nothing.

'It is saying that one person always has to give in. Even this argument is circular. I should give in because then you'll see. But I can't give in because it is so important that you understand.'

'Jen, I ...' He trails off.

There is a silence and I look at him hard, thinking, say it. Over the last few days I've been trying to get him to say a certain phrase to reassure me that I wasn't going mad: 'I am strong, you are strong, and you are not going mad.' I make him say this to me over and over. It is a strange thing to make him say, because by all rational assessments I am mad – but I want him to reassure me that I'm not mad in the way that I fear, that I think most people fear, which is madness in the sense of a complete loss of control, of yourself. Of being so lost that the only solution would be a straitjacket in a padded cell.

'Say it.'

'I am strong, you are strong, and you are not going mad.'

'Say it like you mean it.'

'I do mean it.'

'Say it!'

'I am strong, you are strong and you are not going mad.'

'Say it like you mean it, say it like you mean it, *say it like you mean it*, sayitlikeyoumeanit. SAY IT!'

'I am strong, you are strong, and you are *not* going mad.'

'That's it. I've had enough. You can't even say the one thing I need to hear with conviction!' I shout.

I open the front door and step out onto the landing outside our apartment. We are five storeys up. I flip my leg over the handrail.

'You need to understand how desperate I am, I *need* you to understand me!' I need Kai to understand me, and this seems like the only way to make him see what I mean. To shock him into it. (Looking back, what I *actually* needed was to understand what was happening myself.)

Finally, finally, I push Kai too far. The most patient and loving man I have ever met has reached his limit. He grabs me and pulls me away from the edge.

'Don't do that!' he screams, and pulls me inside the apartment.

'I wasn't going to jump; I just needed you to understand!'

I can see the horror and fury in his face, an expression I have never seen before or since. It pulls me back slightly to reality as he slams the door behind us.

'Never do that again!'

I don't remember this. Kai only told me when I was much better and able to deal with the feeling of horror at what I'd put him through. When he finally did tell me, I was devastated at the fear and pain I must have caused him. He has told me over and over that it wasn't my fault and that he doesn't blame me. But in some sense, the illness is part of me, it came from my brain and my body. I have to take some responsibility for the things I did and the pain I caused.

He decided not to tell any of the health professionals about the moment on the balcony. He says it wasn't like I was really going to jump but that I was just so desperate for him to understand me. He felt that, if he told them, I'd be under even more scrutiny and we were only just coping with two visits a day. Kai doesn't always find it easy to ask for help. Perhaps if he'd told people about this, it would have provided him with more support, but perhaps it could have made things worse. When you are in the middle of a crisis, you have to just keep making decisions and cope the best you can, so I am neither thankful nor angry about his decision.

In desperation, Kai calls my oldest friend in Australia, Lautaro. We were in the same class in school in Hackney, London, and originally made friends through our mutual love of Stephen King books. He is like the brother I never had. He'd moved to Australia a few years before us.

Kai, close to tears, tells Lautaro what has been happening and that he is at the end of his endurance. (I'm in another room at the time, and, like many things, I didn't find out about this until I was much better.)

'We keep on arguing; she won't listen to me and is being more and more aggressive.'

'What can I do to help? Anything at all, just ask.'

'Could you call her and have a chat?'

'Sure, and I'll come and say hello next week.'

Later that day, my phone rings. It is Lautaro. I sit in the rocking chair looking out at the sea and sunshine outside. I pour out all my strange thoughts ... how our friend Justin (my first boyfriend) is Plug One from De La Soul; how it all revolves around pelicans; and how I'm going to write a bestseller (and so is he). We have always had the best conversations, from our teenage chats about the nature of the universe to our mid-thirties chats about – well, the nature of the universe. (We still haven't figured it out yet.)

'Whose book will be best?' he asks, and I laugh. It takes a special skill to talk to someone who is extremely deluded and not get frightened. It takes a special skill to make a joke under those circumstances that makes both of you laugh.

'Mine. But yours will be pretty good too. Like *The Beach* by Alex Garland, only funnier.'

He listens to me with the occasional, "yes I see ..." And "so I hear you saying ..."

He just lets me go on and on, emptying my mind of crazy thoughts and improbable images.

'Jen, if you need anything, you know you just need to ask.'

His voice is calm, just like he always is. He is treating me just as Jen, but Jen who is going through a hard time. Not like a dangerous ill person who needs to be humoured. This is deeply and profoundly relaxing for me, a break from the wary voices I'm used to.

'It is so great to just talk to you. I knew you'd understand.'

'I'll pop by next week, then,' he says.

'See you then.'

*

The next morning, I am peaceful again, and I decide to go for a walk.

'Are you sure you're okay?' Kai asks.

'Yes. I'm feeling much calmer today.'

We hug goodbye and I set off, closing the door of our apartment behind me with a snap.

It is a crisp and beautiful morning and I can feel the stress and strain ebbing away as I walk along the Manly scenic walkway to North Harbour Reserve. I am surrounded by the humming and buzzing of the trees and plants. When I look up, I can see branches leaning over the walkway, swaying in the breeze.

On one tree I see a curled, dried leaf the size of my hand. It is wedged in the crook of a branch, and shaped like a boat washed up against the tree by the tide and the wind. It is filled with rainwater. I stop and marvel – for this is an important Aboriginal artefact! It has probably been resting in the crook of that tree for hundreds of years, filling with rain at every shower and slowly draining away in the hot bright days of years gone by.

Then it hits me: this walkway is probably a sacred Songline for the Aboriginal people who lived around here before white Europeans arrived! (Songlines are also known as "Dreaming tracks". They mark the routes followed by creator-beings during the Dreaming, when the Earth was first made. They are sung from generation to generation, and are like aural maps used to navigate through landmarks, hills, waterholes, and deserts.)

This was the path that my ancestor ran down when she saw Captain Cook's boat! I saw it happen, so it must be true!

The thick undergrowth is a glossy dark green, and the path undulates under my feet as I take step after magical step. The smell of a fragrant jasmine bush transports me back to summer holidays in Cyprus with my family, when the parents let us teenagers camp out at Goat Beach. I am surrounded by beauty, nature at her best.

As I move on, I spy a small nail on the edge of the path. *This nail is from the early convict days*, I think. It is an important artefact and I must collect it and keep it safe. I pick it up and slip it into my pocket. Then I spot a piece of charcoal that is made of burnt bamboo. *Another artefact! How has no one noticed all these important items lying on one of the busiest walkways in Sydney?* By the time I get to the North Harbour Reserve, I have half a dozen items in my pockets and hands.

A large pelican wheels overhead as I go down the steps that lead onto the North Harbour Reserve. She holds her wings steady and rides the thermals.

The reserve is a large expanse of grass, with four great trees and a children's playground. It is bordered on three sides by trees, roads, and houses, and on the fourth by an expanse of mud flats and shallow water. Standing on the grass in the middle of the reserve, I put down my collection of artefacts. I close my eyes and let the breeze play over my outstretched arms.

I wish Kai was with me – he might finally be able to understand. I almost race back to get him, but then realise that it's more important for me to stay standing here with the wind blowing through my body, cleansing me, making my mind clear and focused.

When I sit down, a small dog comes running up to me and drops a ball at my feet. I pick up the ball and throw it back to the owner, but the dog returns to me, dropping the ball again and looking up at me expectantly. I throw the ball again. And again. But the dog comes straight back each time. I point at the ground in front of my feet and the dog drops the ball and it rolls towards me. *I can control this dog with my mind!*

I look around at the four other dogs around the reserve. There are two labradoodles, one golden retriever and one cattle dog. I can control them all if I want to! All around me, the dogs are weaving and running, fetching and returning, making a beautiful pattern over the grass that only I can see.

Inspiration strikes. I work at the Cerebral Palsy Alliance and one of my roles is raising funds for prevention and cure research. We have a team of researchers at our Institute who really believe prevention and cure is possible in our lifetime. One of these researchers is working on mapping the causal pathways of cerebral palsy (this is the special sequence of events that have to happen, in a certain order, for cerebral palsy to occur). One of the causal factors we are looking into is the impact of a bacterial or viral infection in the mother while the baby is in the womb.

Perhaps the infection could come from gum disease? Many people have bleeding gums when they brush their teeth and don't think anything of it, so pregnant women would probably not think to mention it to doctors or anyone looking into the reasons why their child developed cerebral palsy. Maybe this is one of the causal factors and we didn't realise it because we had no data on it!

I'm going to cure cerebral palsy with dental floss. I'll probably get a Nobel Prize for that one. Imagine all the emotional and physical pain that will be avoided once we know that all women have to do is floss to get rid of gum disease while they are pregnant!

What a wonderful thought! I can't wait to ring Iona, Head of Research at the Institute.

I've never felt such peace. I stand up and slowly start walking back home to Kai and my son. With this new calmness, I now know that I will be able to explain everything to Kai.

As I walk back, I notice something strange. Everyone I pass is looking at me, and they look away when I stare back. Two tall and beautiful blonde joggers run towards me. One touches her ear and says something into the hidden microphone. They look away when I smile at them.

I know what's going on.

They must be security laid on by Renée, to protect her from paparazzi and stalkers! That must be why there is so much security around here.

I see a man in sunglasses and a baseball hat, lying on the grass by the side of the path. I see an older but fit-looking couple walking their dog. I see a man kayaking out on the water. All of them are security personnel. All of them.

The day before, I'd seen Manny Devon on the grass in front of our apartment. (Manny was in my year at school in Hackney. He has large, beautiful eyes and dark, smooth skin – we'd all had a crush on him back in those days.) He was pretending to give personal training to a woman who was also part of his team. I stared at them until they both smiled up at me.

I'd been messaging him on Facebook. He must have thought it was so funny being in touch with me, pretending to be back in London, when he was actually in Australia. I can tell from the photos on Facebook that he is now running a personal security company for very high-profile clients. But the number of bodyguards around does seem a bit much for just one famous actress ...

When I get back, I find Kai watching a World Cup rugby match with our son, who is gurgling on his mat. I tuck myself in next to him on the sofa after I've made both of us a cup of tea. He is watching the match intently, so I'll explain things to him later.

I'm on Facebook that evening as Kai baths and feeds our boy and gets him to bed. I'm looking at the homepage of Jackle, a kid in our class at school. He has a picture of Barack Obama shaking hands with someone. I stare at the picture and the other person starts to wobble and fade. I realise that, in the future, the person is going to turn into me.

That is why there is so much security around! Barack Obama is coming to meet me!

Renée has organised it. But why? I can't work it out for the life of me. I look over at Kai, who is sitting in the rocking chair and feeding our son his bottle. He has a faraway expression as he gently rocks back and forth, murmuring to the baby in Norwegian. I decide not to tell him – it can be a surprise.

We have arranged to Skype with my parents at seven o'clock, just before a scheduled visit from the Extended Hours Team (we – or mainly Kai – think it will alleviate some of the anxiety for my parents if we Skype all together – Mum and Dad can then ask questions if needed). I load up the application. I can't wait to tell them everything! They'll be so pleased.

My parents' faces fill the screen, and they coo and wave when Kai holds my son up to the webcam.

'Hello,' I say, as Kai takes the baby off to bed. Then I notice that there are curtains behind them I don't recognise. 'Where are you?'

'At the cottage,' Mum tells me.

'I don't recognise the curtains.'

'We usually Skype in the kitchen, but we're in the sitting room this morning.'

I don't believe her.

'Where are you really?' I ask.

Mum sets her lips into a straight line. 'We are at the cottage,' she repeats. 'Really, love.'

Then it hits me. *They are in Australia!* They are downstairs in Emily's flat. Renée had been talking to Lindsay Lohan, and they thought it would be a lovely surprise if my parents were around to meet Obama too. After all, I'm the person I am today because of my parents.

'Are you downstairs?' I demand.

'No.' Dad frowns, his brow furrowed. 'We really are at the cottage.'

I guess they don't want to spoil the surprise, so I go along with them.

A few weeks ago, my sister, Jo, had sent me a present. It was a 1956 edition of *The Sea Around Us* by Rachel Carson (best known for sparking the environmental movement with her seminal book, *Silent Spring*).

'Hey, guess what?' I ask. 'Jo sent me a really marvellous present.'

'Did she?'

'Yeah, it's by a really famous author. I think it might be worth a lot of money. I've emailed Christies' rare book department and they are getting back to me with a valuation.'

'Jen!' says Mum, shocked.

'Don't you think Jo will be so pleased once I find out exactly how much it is worth? I think it is probably worth at least a million pounds.'

The room darkens as the sun slips below Balgowlah Heights to the west. My parents are silent.

'I'll go and get it,' I tell them.

Going over to the bookcase, I gently slide the book in question off the shelf. Next to it, I see another book: *Lucky Jim* by Kingsley Amis. "*Lucky Jim*", I think. *My dad's called Jim.*

I stare at the cover picture, which is a line-drawing of a man standing in front of a Cambridge college and holding two books:

Toynbee and *A Short History of Economic Theory*. It looks exactly like Dad.

This means this book is worth a lot of money too. *This is so exciting! I wonder how Dad will like being famous once everyone finds out Lucky Jim is based on him.*

'How are you?' my mum asks Kai, back at the computer. She knows first-hand how hard it is to look after someone with delusions.

'Okay. Pretty tired.'

'Here it is.' I wave the Rachel Carson book in front of the camera. 'But I've just made another discovery. Dad, have you read the book *Lucky Jim*?'

'Yes. I studied it in school, in fact.'

'I have a copy here, and I think it's based on you, Dad.'

They both laugh out loud.

'I'm serious! Look at the picture, it looks just like you.'

'No, Jen, that's not possible. I studied it at school, so it was published when I was a boy. It couldn't be based on me, I'm too young.'

'But it must be you.'

'It can't be, Jen.'

'Have you read it?' asks Mum.

'No, not yet.'

'Then how do you know it is based on Dad?'

'Why won't you believe me? Why won't you all just believe what I say for once? It is so exhausting!'

Mum and Dad glance at each other. Then my mum leans forward towards Kai, who's sitting next to me.

'You must call for help. Call for help *now*.'

Suddenly, there is a knock at the door. It is Jane and Sandra, and we invite them in, explaining that we are already Skyping with my parents.

'We thought it would alleviate some of the anxiety for Jen's parents if we Skyped all together, then they can ask you questions,' Kai explains.

My mind is racing – not only am I meeting Obama, but I can introduce my parents to the team, and they'll see how well I'm doing! **What a fantastic idea!**

They pull a bench up to the desk so that we're sitting in a horseshoe around the laptop.

'How are you doing today, Jen?' asks Jane.

'I'm okay but I did have quite a weird experience earlier today.'

'What was that?'

'I went for a walk and everyone was looking at me, but looked away when I looked at them. They were all security personnel for tomorrow.'

'What is happening tomorrow?'

They are calm and neutral. Just asking a normal question in a normal conversation.

'I'm sure you know. No need to pretend.' I brush them off. I'm getting exasperated.

'No, I'm afraid we don't. Could you tell us?' Sandra smiles gently at me.

'Oh, and I found this book that my sister gave me, and I think it is worth a lot of money.'

'Jen,' says Jane firmly, 'what do you think is going to happen tomorrow?'

'We are going to meet Obama. Together we are going to use Facebook to catch all paedophiles.'

There is silence.

'Jen,' says my mum, 'lots of strange things are happening to you. But if you – and I mean both of you – want me to come out, I will.'

'I think we'll be okay,' I reassure her. 'Once everyone finally understands what I'm trying to explain, I think everything will be great. You'll see.'

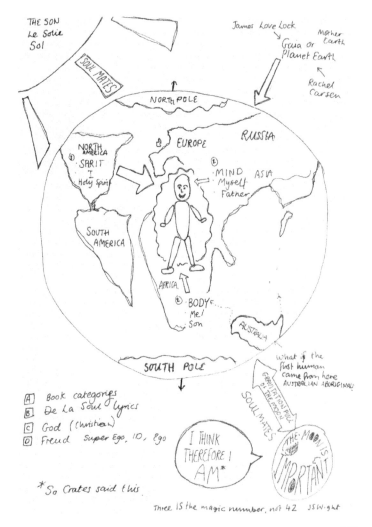

Sandra and Jane sit and talk with my parents, answering questions about what is happening to me. I barely register the conversation. Somewhere, underneath it all, I have a vague awareness that they are helping my parents deal with the difficult situation of seeing me so ill and being so far away. *Another daughter going mad*. On some level, I know how awful that must be. But as I gaze out of the window, I start to daydream about how fantastic it will be not having to worry about any child ever being abused ever again – and that's more important.

After a while, I drift back into the room and I ask for my medication.

'I want to take it in front of my parents so they can see.'

They flip open the black briefcase and take out two boxes. They pop four tablets out of their blister packs and hand them over to me. One olanzapine, one temazepam and two of an anti-convulsant called sodium valproate which is used to treat epilepsy, as well as a mood stabiliser. They started me on it earlier in the week.

'Look,' I say to my parents, 'I'm being compliant.'

'Good,' laughs Mum.

'Well done,' Dad tells me.

'Jen, I can see you are being very well looked after,' says Mum.

'Yes, everyone has been very kind. Though sometimes people stay too long.' I smile pointedly at Jane.

'That's our cue, I think,' agrees Jane.

'Lovely to meet you,' says Mum. 'And thanks for looking after our daughter so well.'

After we've finished talking to Mum and Dad, and Jane and Sandra have left, Kai and I sit on the sofa tucking into another takeaway meal.

'It will be okay, you know that?' he says.

'With you by my side everything is possible,' I reply.

CHAPTER 15

THERE'S A WORLD WITHIN ME THAT I CANNOT EXPLAIN

Saturday dawns bright. I am starting to catch up with sleep and feel more rested.

'How are you today?' asks Kai.

'Okay. I feel less tired, but I'm still having such strange thoughts.'

'Sorry to hear that.'

He has dark circles under his puffy eyes. I feel a stab of guilt – I know that me catching up on my sleep means he is getting less.

After our morning visit from the Extended Hours Team, I make a cup of tea. The flat is peaceful and quiet – but then I hear a sound coming from my son's room.

Kai is sitting on the day bed with his face in his hands. He is crying quietly.

'What's wrong?'

'They said ...' he begins, but falters.

'I'm so sorry." I apologise and sit down beside him. "You must be exhausted.' I put my arms around him and rest my cheek against his.

'It's not that. I mean, yes, I'm knackered; it's just ... last week they said ... they said that you might be a risk to our boy!'

This terrible thought moves from him to me and swirls in with all the other unbelievable things that are happening to us. My frantic, overworked brain holds the information at arm's length while it whirrs and tries to process it all.

No, no, not me, not me. I would never, never, NEVER ...

I quickly file the thought away in the "things too hard to think about now" file. My priority in this moment is Kai, and the pain he is in. He dissolves into crying again, and I hug him tight. (In among all the madness, all the strange thoughts and feelings, I still had enough of "me" left to know that, no, I would never harm my son.)

'I didn't know whether to tell you or not,' he admits.

'I don't think I'm a risk' is the only reassurance I can give him.

'No, not when you're like this, but when you are in a bad place, you just ... we just ... I don't know how much more I can take.'

We sit in silence, holding tightly to one another. Kai takes a deep breath and wipes the tears from his eyes.

'It is just so hard,' he concludes, and my heart turns to lead in my chest.

'This is all my fault.'

'No. It isn't anyone's fault; it's just so hard. Tell you what, let's make the most of you feeling okay and go and get a coffee, okay? I can start talking really fast!'

Kai is a coffee lover. I love that he loves coffee because when he has one, he starts talking nineteen to the dozen about all and everything. After a coffee, my normally "glass-half-full" husband takes optimism to a new level, putting the bound into boundless, and he is a delight to be around.

So, we load up the buggy and brave the steepness of Woods Parade. At the top of the hill is the little row of shops that makes up Fairlight's main road. There is a butcher's, a café, pharmacist, bottle shop, grocer, dry cleaner and a little bakery. The butcher's shop has a café attached and tables out on the pavement. We sit down at the one free table. The other tables throng with families with golden-haired children. They squeal and play around us with the sun glinting off their shining heads. I smile at Kai, who smiles back and starts playing with my son.

'Where's Papa? Here's Papa!'

A cloud passes over the sun and the shining heads dim to shade. A cooler breeze puffs along the row of shops. A man with long dark hair pulled back into a stringy ponytail is walking backwards and forwards along the pavement. He is sauntering slowly, rolling each foot down, with his hands clasped behind his back. As he walks, he looks at each child. His face is blank.

A chill creeps up from my stomach. *Something is very wrong with this man.*

'Look at him,' I say.

'Who?'

'That man. What is he doing?'

'He does look a bit suss,' Kai laughs.

'He is scoping out those children. We have to warn them.'

'No, I think he works here – look, he's wearing an apron.'

'That's probably what he wants people to think.'

I stand up and start towards the mother on the next table, but Kai grabs my hand.

'No, Jen.'

'But we have to.'

'No, please. Look, he's stopped now.'

The man has walked into the café and is leaning against the edge of the counter, acting as if he works there – but I know he's just pretending.

'But he's a paedophile!' I hiss.

'No, Jen, he isn't. Time to go.'

Kai starts to lead me away across the road and back down Woods Parade.

'Jen. It's okay. Don't worry. Nothing bad is going to happen.'

We are halfway down the road when I stop and turn to go back.

'I have to do something!'

Kai puts a strong arm around my shoulders turning me back around.

'He is evil, I know it.'

'No, Jen, he isn't.' Kai pulls me into a tight hug. 'Trust me.'

Then a taxi drives past.

'Look a police car!' I exclaim.

'No, Jen, that's a taxi.'

I give him a disbelieving look and start waving at the car.

'Jen! It's a taxi.'

Then I remember the security staff from Manny Devon's company who are watching over us. **Manny will catch him. They will know what to do with him. Manny's company are pulling out all the stops to make sure I'm safe. Barack Obama and me. We are going to use Facebook to get all paedophiles!** I am brimming over with joy. I see a huge safety net spanning the world with paedophiles all caught in it, and all the children of the world are safe. I might even get a knighthood! I know that isn't the point of it, but I think my parents would be so proud of me.

'S'okay,' I say to Kai. 'Manny will take care of it.'

He flashes me a crooked smile but has stopped asking me

what I mean. I let him lead me and the buggy back home.

Later that day we sit in the living room: me and Kai, Peter, Clare / Lindsay Lohan and their son Hugo. My son is napping in his bassinet. I look at Peter. *He is a millionaire, and we didn't even know it!* He's kept it hidden so well. He looks relaxed and happy as we sit and chat idly.

Something amazing is about to happen; I can tell from the way Peter and Clare / Lindsay seem full to bursting with some exciting news. They aren't ready to tell us yet. *If Kai would only shut up and give them the space they need to tell us whatever it is!*

I get a flash of inspiration. *I know what it is! Peter is going to give my charity, Cerebral Palsy Alliance, one million dollars!* He's been so impressed with what I've told him about how the charity is run and what excellent work we do that he's decided to make his first major gift to us. *This is amazing!* I imagine that, after they've told us, I will ring my boss, Mike, and put him on speakerphone so that he can hear for himself. *Between us — me, Peter, and the researchers I work with — we really might find a cure for cerebral palsy. We really might!* I give Peter a huge smile.

'So, how've you been?' asks Clare / Lindsay.

'It has been very weird, and I've had all these strange thoughts. I thought I was Cameron Diaz earlier this week.'

We all laugh.

'And I thought you were Lindsay Lohan,' I tell Clare / Lindsay. *Still do.*

She almost jumps out of her seat.

'No – really?' she exclaims, but I've already turned to Peter.

'I think I might be part of a group of people who find a cure for cerebral palsy!'

Peter is leaning back with his hands behind his head. His eyes are brimming with tears. It's no wonder – giving that much money away to a charity is very emotional!

'And I thought that I was going to be able to use Facebook to catch all ...' I pause and my voice catches, '... all the paedophiles in the world.'

Kai looks at me sharply. I decide not to say anything about Obama as I don't want to spoil their surprise.

My chin sinks to my chest in the silence that follows my proclamation. Then we hear the waking squeaks of my son, and I go into his room to pick him up.

I think about Peter-the-secret-millionaire while I'm changing The Boy's nappy. *He must have met Lindsay Lohan in London and fallen in love. Together they relocated to Sydney to get away from the paparazzi* ... This thought echoes through my consciousness, trying to find a place to rest. *Peter, who always thought people would see the money first and the man second, and Clare / Lindsay, who had been so traumatised by her child-stardom and crackers parents ...*

I bring our baby back into the room and Kai suggests we go for a walk.

He keeps talking and won't give Peter the chance he needs to raise the subject. *Come on, be quiet!* He walks on ahead with Peter, and I walk with Clare / Lindsay. *If I let her know that I know about Renée Zellweger being in the building, she might open up ...*

'... And she's staying with her mum in the ground-floor flat of our building.'

'You must write this stuff down,' she says.

'Oh, I will. I'm going to write a book about it.'

As we walk up the path where it joins with Lauderdale Avenue, Clare / Lindsay quickly pulls her sunglasses down and sweeps her hair around to cover her face. *Poor thing,* I think. *She's so used to hiding, she does it automatically.*

As we return from our walk, we pass Emily's flat.

'This one,' I whisper to Clare / Lindsay. She smiles awkwardly and whisks Peter and Hugo away.

No matter, I think, *maybe it's best they announce it tomorrow.*

*

And this was one of the better days. On the bad days, Kai and I would just argue and argue. One day it was because I thought he had a photographic memory. My conviction grew from the fact that he has a good memory, and I kept on battering him until he just agreed with me. It usually happened like that. The arguments would go on and on, until we were exhausted and he would have to agree with me. Otherwise, the arguments would never end.

I have experienced delusions, and I know the utter conviction they bring. I believed them all to be true. They overrode my normal perspectives of: "each to their own", "agree to disagree", and "each person creates their own truth". And they turned me into a belligerent, dogmatic bully.

The insights I got from my own experiences helped give me much more understanding of my sister's difficult behaviour surrounding her own delusional beliefs. It didn't and doesn't make them any easier to deal with, but now, at least I feel as if I understand her experience.

CHAPTER 16

CHARLEY SAYS, 'ALWAYS TELL YOUR MUMMY.'

My son is fast asleep and I'm pacing back and forth.

'Something is wrong, I just know it.'

'It's okay, Jen. Time for us to go to sleep.'

'One in four children is abused. Did you know that?'

'Yes, you told me.'

I'd been horrified to learn of this statistic at work training. Because people with disability are at a higher risk of abuse, everyone who works at the Cerebral Palsy Alliance takes part in training around preventing, and responding to, abuse. I'm not sure why the thought came to me in that moment; it felt like I suddenly had access to every piece of information I had ever known. My conscious mind was elevated to a higher level of performance, filtering over and over again every memory, every thought, every feeling.

'One in four,' I say again. As I pace, I go through a list of everyone I know, stopping at each fourth person: *Harry, Kingsley, Gareth, Kitty, Anne, Ned, Timmy, Paul.*

'It's so awful. I can hardly stand it.'

Tears are streaming down my face. All these friends were abused! How could something so terrible happen?

But then I have a sudden thought that twists my stomach.

'I think I was abused,' I say to Kai. 'I think I may have suppressed the memory.'

'I don't think so, Jen. You're just having lots of strange thoughts at the minute.'

'Oh, God, I think I know who did it, who abused all of us! It was Brian – you know Brian, one of my parents' friends? He had us all in his basement! I'd always been uncomfortable around him. Now I know why!'

'But, Jen, don't you think your parents wouldn't be friends with him anymore if that had happened? In fact, he'd be in jail if you'd been in his basement.'

'You don't understand!'

'I know, that's the point.'

I get my phone and write a text to my parents: *Brian is a paedo*.

I sit looking at the words on the screen.

'Jen, you've got to get some sleep.'

'How can I sleep with all this going on?'

I look back at the text, but something is stopping me from sending it. I know it's urgent; Brian needs to be stopped. He might even have children in the basement now! The more I delay, the longer they have to suffer.

But I don't send the text. Some part of me knows it isn't true. My motley crew of friends and I were not abused. Brian is, in fact, a lovely, kind man who would never hurt a child – or anyone, for that matter. The thought of the pain this would cause my parents if they received the text is like a hand reaching down through the water of confusion in which I'm drowning, cupping my chin and turning my face to the surface to see the light of reason above. I can't get to it, but I know it's there above me.

But the feeling of evil, the delusion – as I know it to be later – is so strong after that man outside the butcher's café and now Brian.

Kai eventually goes to bed, and I sit up playing on Facebook.

I look at the text to my parents one more time as I turn off the computer. But I still don't send it. At the core of me, under layer upon layer of manic madness, I'm still in control. Deep down, I know not to send it.

This control doesn't stop me from wondering if I'll be able to sleep though, not when I know that I'm going to meet Obama tomorrow. The promise of seeing Obama is always "tomorrow". It's like a doomsday cult, always recalculating the end of days. My brain is like the White Queen promising Alice jam: "the rule is, jam tomorrow and jam yesterday – but never jam today."

The day had to keep shifting by a day to keep the delusion true. All else must be sacrificed to keep the delusion true: rationality, truth, love.

Because if the delusion isn't real, then I truly must be mad.

*

The next day is Sydney-special: clear blue sky, the odd puff of cloud, and warm, balmy temperatures. I remember the text message as soon as I wake up, and a chill goes down my spine. I grab my phone and check drafts, and there it is. *Phew*. I delete the text. Imagine if I'd sent that to my parents!

I know, this morning, that I am wrong. It is a relief to be back in my right mind, away from the frantic confusion of the delusions. Sometimes in movies you see a fight scene where the baddy is holding the hero's head under water. The hero struggles and fights, holding her breath. Then the baddy pulls her head out of the water. She gasps for breath, water running down her face. She doesn't have much time to think or plan. All she can do is take in the precious breath. The lucid moments were like that, vital for my survival, vital for me to try to process what was happening to me, but they never felt long enough for a real break from the horror.

The conviction that I'm going to meet Obama fades. I think back to knowing Peter was going to give us one million dollars and it all seems so unlikely. And how can Clare be Lindsay Lohan when she is Clare? Like the water on the hero's face, the madness and delusions temporarily rinse away, leaving me cold and rational.

The day passes with bottles, feeds, nappies, and calmness. Kai and I don't argue, and everything seems to be returning to normal.

At three o'clock, Lautaro comes around and we head out to the North Harbour Reserve to meet our friends, Mark and Beth, and their daughter, Katie. Lautaro, Mark, and I kick a football back and forth between us while Kai chats to Beth, and Mark's mum, and Katie plays on the seesaw.

I spot a dog in the distance and stop speaking mid-sentence. The dog is running towards us in great bounds. I frown at it. I manage to pull myself back from the brink.

I can't control the dog with my mind, I think.

'Do you want to sit down?' asks Lautaro.

And so we sit on the grass a little away from the others and I carry on telling him about what has been happening. He listens and nods, telling me it sounds scary. Telling me I've always been headstrong. That I can cope. It feels good to talk to him again.

Sunday turns to Monday, and then to Tuesday, but despite Sunday's upturn, I get worse and worse with more delusions. One night I think I may have killed a man at university who tried to rape me – another suppressed memory of something that never happened. I spend hours watching De La Soul videos on YouTube.

I write pages and pages of equations and scribbles.

Watch Bridget Jones's Diary + Anne of Green Gables + Goodnight Mr Tom + Mr Men + Cranford + Jane Austin + Muppets + Jim Henderson + Eric Carle + Guy Date Chain (choker) + Guy on Table + Boxer + Joe is Christopher Robin + Peter Pan. Sainsbury's + Ginger Guy. May FDP + Olly + Grandpa Jim. Toy Snail + Friends + Magic Roundabout.

Being Weird + McDonald's = Dad = Lucky Jim

$Jim + j + I = m$

$I + j = m$

$m + Castro = I$

Diary of a Wimpy Kid

Sarah + Michael + He is my brother

He ain't heavy

$H + e = I$

Bill is me + William = Bunce

Bill + am = teacher

Jo is my sister

Teffa = Judy 1

Tuffa + Judy 2 = Kath

Kath Kelly + Fred = ?

Our Willy = Our Willie

The Browns = Kill

$K + I = Kill I am$

K Dora = Scrabble

Monopoly + bull bars = Dead kid.

One day I have a mini shopping spree at our local mall in Balgowlah. I'm convinced that the items for sale in a clothes shop are based on treasures rescued from the Titanic – but what they don't realise is that they've included the original relics by mistake. *This is so exciting! I don't want to give the game away, though ...* I riffle through the racks to find the "original" items, and buy bags and necklaces like they're going out of fashion. It's the same story in the shop next door. I buy some white enamel doorknobs with "IN" and "OUT" on them, convinced they are the very doorknobs from the kitchens on the Titanic.

That night Kai and I have a marathon argument – there's not even really a subject; we're so exhausted and I'm getting so irritated by every irrational thing that it doesn't take much to spark a row these days. I start to experience a feeling like I am not in control of my body. I am terrified about holding my son, fearing I may drop him if my arms aren't under my control.

Eventually we both collapse in bed, both of us completely drained. Then Kai starts to cry.

The lack of control I'm feeling fades away. My body calms down and I kneel next to Kai on the bed, holding him tightly as he cries and cries.

'I'm so sorry. So sorry,' I tell him.

'I can't stand the arguing anymore,' he sobs.

'I know. I'm sorry.'

Slowly, he manages to calm down and stop crying. He lies there making small movements. *What is he doing?*

'What's happening? Are you okay?'

'I'm just doing that relaxation technique – you know the one, when I tense a part of my body and then relax it.'

'I think you're having a panic attack.'

'No, Jen, I'm doing this on purpose.'

'That's what you think.'

'Please, Jen. Please no more.'

He stops, and I lie down next to him, holding him tight again.

'Have you ever had a panic attack before?'

I'm met with silence. Eventually, we both drop off into fitful sleep.

*

Kai has to take another week off work. The Extended Hours Team start talking about options.

'Hospital,' says Jane, and my heart seizes for a second, freezing my blood and closing my chest.

I'm not Jo; I can't go to a psychiatric unit!

'No, no – I can't go to hospital!'

'It's just an option.'

'I'm going mad!' I sob, covering my face in my hands. The tears run down my palms.

'No, Jen, you've got something caused by pregnancy and the birth. You haven't got schizophrenia. You will get 100% better, this much we know.'

'Really? Really?'

'Yes, without doubt. But you need some help right now,' Jane implores me.

'It would be more for me than you, really, Jen. I don't know how much longer I can carry on,' says Kai, heavily.

This hits me. Hard.

It takes a lot for Kai to admit this. As well as looking after me in my confused, hallucinating, deluded, and highly irritable state, Kai has taken most responsibility for looking after my son. Trying to keep up with me, and keep on top of things in the house, has taken its toll. We've had takeaway every night in the last week, and I've been in such a state that I've not really realised how much work Kai has been doing just to keep our heads above water.

When I think of this now, I'm so grateful for having Kai as a boyfriend, then husband, and then co-parent. There aren't many people who would have put up with the extreme stresses my illness has put on our relationship. I am and always will be extremely grateful to him. Through everything we went through, he never blamed me, he only ever blamed the illness. I may not always have been able to do the same, but he did.

'We've got you an appointment on Monday with Dr Mortimer – you met him earlier this week,' says Jane. 'He will assess whether you need to go into hospital or not.'

'Will I get sectioned?'

The word seems to echo around the room. *Sectioned. Sectioned. Sectioned.*

I picture the first locked unit the doctors put my sister in when she was 18 – the thick door with the small pane of reinforced glass, the TV bolted high in the corner of the lounge, the stink of fear and confusion that had built up over many years in the layers of grime on the walls. My sister's smooth, beautiful face smothered with layers of fat, her skin turning pasty and grey and her bright, lively brain smashed by illness, medication smothering what was left.

My sister. Me. My sister. Me. We always looked so alike, despite the three-year age gap.

'Jen, no – you would be a voluntary patient.'

After they leave, I start crying again. My eyes are squeezed shut and the tears are building up under my eyelids. When I open my eyes, a flood of tears washes my face.

'I can't go to hospital! What am I going to do?'

Kai hugs me close and we get ready for settling my son for the night.

CHAPTER 17

FOR IT'S MUCH TOO LATE TO GET AWAY OR TURN ON THE LIGHT

The next day, we are sitting in the reception of the adult mental health unit in Manly Hospital, waiting for our appointment with Dr Mortimer. I'm clutching a photograph of my sister and me. I don't know why, but I need it with me today. The woman behind reception smiles at Kai as he takes my son out of his buggy and jiggles him on his knee.

A young man of 18 or 19 comes and sits in the reception area. He is wearing a grey T-shirt and grey jogging bottoms with flip-flops. He has peach plasters wrapped around each toe, contrasting against his brown skin. He has some tobacco, papers, a lighter, and loose change in a clear zip-lock plastic bag. He is looking over at The Boy. I beam at him. His eyes are wide, and he nervously looks away.

'Hello,' I say and his smile flicks on for a moment and then is gone. He reminds me so much of my sister; not in looks, but the way he holds his body slow and still as if waiting for a punch, and the confused, frightened blinking of his eyes.

'I love kids,' he mutters, slowly fumbling in the bag. I feel a great surge of protectiveness towards him.

I tell him my son's name.

'That's a good name,' the young man approves, extracting the tobacco and papers. He starts to roll a cigarette. *He has schizophrenia, I just know it*. His hands tremble slightly as he puts the rollie between his lips. 'Nice name,' he repeats as he stands and starts to walk out the door.

'Hey,' I call after him, and I hold up the picture of my sister and me. 'You will get better, you know.'

He stops and turns back, a big smile transforming his frozen face.

'I just know it,' I tell him again, holding the photograph forward so he can see.

'Thanks,' he says. He pushes the door open and steps outside. 'Thanks.'

I sit and look at the photograph. In it, my arm is around Jo's shoulder. *Maybe that's why I'm meeting this senior doctor, why this is happening to me. I'm going to cure schizophrenia! With my insight and personal experience, and his knowledge and connections, between us we are going to cure schizophrenia.* A bolt of pure happiness passes through me. *My sister – I am going to cure her! She can come and live with us in Australia. She is going to get better!*

My eyes fill with tears of happiness. *I can cure someone by just telling a person they are going to be okay! It is all so clear now. They believe me because I'm right, and the placebo effect does the rest. All I need to do is fly back to England and tell my sister she is going to get better and she will.*

'It's all going to be okay,' I say to Kai.

He looks up at me with a smile. 'It's good you feel like that.'

Tianna, from the Extended Hours Team, comes to collect us and we enter Dr Mortimer's office.

He is sitting at his desk and gets up to greet us as we file into the room. He's a tall man with a closely cropped beard. He is wearing a shirt with thin purple stripes and gold sun cuff links.

Kai manoeuvres the buggy into a corner and we all sit down. Dr Mortimer and Tianna are watching me.

'How are you, Jen?' asks the doctor.

'I've been better, to be honest, Dr Mortimer.' I hold out the photograph. 'I know I've got to show you this, but I don't know why? It's my sister.'

'Can you tell me what's been happening?' he asks.

I explain about the man the day before, and the fact that I think I'm going to cure cerebral palsy and schizophrenia. I tell him about Cameron Diaz, Lindsay Lohan, and the repressed memories of abuse and attempted rape. I also tell them about what I thought was Kai's panic attack, but they don't seem to worry about that.

As I talk, Dr Mortimer slumps further and further down in his seat, his hands steepled as he listens with a serious face. He is now so low that he's practically lying down in the chair with his legs splayed open. His bottom lip curls over and droops down his chin, the skin under his eyes melting until I can almost see his cheekbones. It looks so funny that I start to laugh.

Kai has been talking, but now he looks over at me.

'He looks so funny,' I laugh, looking back at Dr Mortimer, who is now sitting upright in his chair.

Kai, Tianna, and Dr Mortimer are all staring at me, and I feel my eyes starting to shut.

'I'm so tired.' I giggle, looking again at Dr Mortimer. **His face must be made of rubber,** I think, stifling another giggle. I can feel myself sliding sideways out of the chair. I'm so tired that I drop into sleep. I'm going to fall off, and a great bubble of laughter swells in my chest. Then I remember the young man outside. I open my eyes and sit up in the chair.

'I met a man in the reception and I know he has schizophrenia. How could I know that?'

'Well, this is a mental health unit. It is a good bet that he has schizophrenia or a related illness.'

'He had plasters around his toes.'

They both smile in recognition and I think, *I'm right*.

'I told him he was going to get better.'

'Why?'

'Because he'll believe me and that will make all the difference.'

'But back to you, Jen,' says Dr Mortimer, and the questions continue.

By the end of the meeting, it is agreed that I will be going to a perinatal mental health unit in Hornsby. This is a special unit specifically for new mums who are having serious mental health problems. We can stay with my son, unlike in more traditional units where the mother and baby would be separated. Even Kai can stay with us in the hospital. We are due to be admitted the following day.

Hospital. I am going to hospital.

But they very much make it feel like it is our decision, Kai's and mine. I feel like I'm on a conveyor belt in a vast factory, moving towards a huge machine. The belt goes into the machine through a dark rectangle. I can't see inside the machine, but I can hear clanking and stamping and hisses of steam. Around me are friendly faces, encouraging me. I've climbed onto the conveyor belt myself. I know I have to, for my sake as much as Kai's, but I'm terrified as I move closer to the machine and the belt ahead of me is swallowed up by the darkness. *I must do this. I have to.*

CHAPTER 18

SHE'S A MANIAC, MANIAC ON THE FLOOR

The Moon is Important.

My diary entry.

'I'm going to throw up. Throw up!'

I'm crouching by the side of the bed. We are in the Perinatal Mental Health Unit of St Anne Hospital in Hornsby.

'Here, take this,' says Magda, one of the nurses. She hands me a sick bag.

'Too small, I need to get to the bathroom.'

'Probably best if you stay here,' she argues.

'Help me,' I beg Kai. He grabs my hand and, ignoring Magda, helps me to the en-suite bathroom.

Just in time, I drop to my knees by the toilet, heaving and gasping. It feels like the whole contents of my stomach evacuate in a stream of vomit as wide as my open mouth. My stomach heaves three more times before the nausea passes, and I have to gulp as I sit back on my heels.

I lean forward again with my arm draped around the seat. Kai and Magda are standing in the door of the bathroom. Kai is looking down at me. Magda is looking down on me. Even through all my confusion, I can feel the difference in their gazes.

We'd arrived earlier in the day, Friday, with bags packed for a week's stay.

It's a long weekend, and everyone we passed on the way to the hospital seemed to be bustling along, packing their cars with beach chairs and frisbees in preparation. We have no such frisson of future pleasure expected.

Kai had been quiet in the car on the way over.

'You okay?' I asked.

'I was just about to ask you the same thing. You're very quiet.'

'I'm shitting myself.'

'You are strong, I am strong. And you are not going mad.'

'Thank you.' A pause. 'God, I made you say that so many times ...'

'I know, but it's true – that's why I kept saying it.'

In the car, I sat and thought about how scared I was about being in a mental hospital. I was picturing padded cells and straitjackets. Electrodes being attached to my head, electricity scrambling my brain. My freedom taken from me. The madness itself stealing my very essence. For, what are you if not the sum total of your thoughts, feelings, and memories? You are your mind. And if your mind is wrapped in layer after layer of lies and delusions that it is telling itself, where are you? I'll tell you. You are gone. You die temporarily while your body continues.

I think this is why psychosis – what some consider "true" madness – is one of the more feared mental illnesses. It is a type of living death. You lose yourself. Your loved ones don't know how to treat the mindless body that so resembles their friend, their daughter, their wife. It isn't surprising many people respond with fear or create distance. To literally and figuratively remove themselves from the ill person's orbit. Don't contact, don't visit, don't write, don't email. Don't even think of them. It is too painful or difficult for them.

When I was in the mother and baby unit, my work sent me a bunch of flowers wishing me a speedy recovery. I was very touched and comforted by this. Whoever organised it, I realise, wanted to treat my illness normally. In hindsight, I realise this was a significant gesture; after talking to my network of friends who have experienced PPP, I discovered that, unlike sufferers of physical illnesses, most women with PPP don't receive flowers or get-well cards when they are ill.

But back to the journey. We arrived at a long, low building with a statue of St Anne out the front in a round raised flowerbed. She had a small child in her arms. We were shown to our room. It is just outside the staff room, so if it is anything like the hospital where my son was born, we are going to have disturbed nights. Well, even more disturbed nights than you get with an eight-week-old baby, at least. The room is clean and sparsely furnished with a double bed, wardrobe, rocking chair, and a changing table, all plain and sturdy. The only decoration is a wooden crucifix with a carved Jesus dying painfully on the wall above the door. The little en suite has a walk-in shower, basin, and toilet. There were thin, but clean, white towels folded over a towel rail. I was relieved to see that it was a fairly normal room. Apart from the crucifix.

Kai unpacked while I sat on the bed and played with my son. At twelve o'clock, we decided to head upstairs to the dining room for lunch. My unit is one of many at St Anne Hospital, and the dining room was starting to fill up with other patients. I scanned the room, wondering about the stories of all these people. A young girl, painfully thin, sat with her mother and sister. An older man with a wide face and big square glasses was sitting on his own. There were two other mothers in the room with their buggies drawn up next to their tables. *They must be from my ward*.

We filled up on soup, a selection of salads and a roll. The salads are "serve yourself" from a metal unit on wheels, the compartments of salads lit by an overhead lamp. One of the salads tasted a bit funny so, after eating a few mouthfuls, I pushed it to the side.

*

I think back to that salad while I'm hanging off the toilet seat.

'Food poisoning,' I gasp, unable to manage the demands of proper sentence structure.

'Most likely this is linked to your psychosis,' says Magda, clinically. I feel so nauseous I don't really register the word. Psychosis.

'Really?' asks Kai. They both stand there looking at me.

'I think the worst of it is out,' I announce.

'Come on, Jen.' Kai holds out his hand, helps me to my feet, then guides me back to bed.

But as I lie there on the mattress, my arms and legs start to spasm.

'I'm not in control of my body,' I whisper through clenched teeth.

Kai crouches down by the side of the bed holding my hands. 'It is going to be okay,' he assures me earnestly.

Magda stands behind him, clasping her hands together.

The room is contracting and releasing.

'I'm going,' I say desperately.

'You are safe here. I'm here. Everything is going to be okay,' Kai tells me. But the room contracts and releases then fades to nothing, and the double bed disappears …

I realise I am kneeling next to a hard, thin mattress on a canvas cot. My hands are clasped together. I am praying. Tears are streaming down my face.

'Please forgive me, Lord, for my sin,' I pray. I am

looking up at the crucifix through a blur of tears. I feel soiled and dirty. I get to my feet and lift the heavy material of my cassock above my head. I am standing naked by the washstand.

Back in the room, Magda and Kai watch my arms and legs jerking and twitching.

I sluice my face with water, then wash under my arms and between my legs. I feel a penis, limp and rubbery, between my hands.

Why would God test me like this? Why would He put so much temptation in my path? I try to block the images of kissing my fellow monk, his tongue, his stubble rough on my lips, his hands on my hips pulling me close. How can something so full of the worst sin feel so full of beauty?

I thought my love for him was the love of a brother, until this morning when a few minutes of weakness had led me to commit one of the worst sins imaginable. How can I go on here at the monastery?

I roughly dry myself and pull my cassock back over my head. I return to my spot on the floor by the cot and start to pray again. It must all be part of God's plan for me. He is testing my faith, knowing I will fail, to teach me humility. God is good. He loves me but hates my sin. I lean forward with my head resting on my clasped hands. I continue to pray and I can feel the cold floor chilling my knees and shins through my cassock.

The room shimmers and warps again, and Kai appears in my vision. He is kneeling close to me.

'I'm okay,' I tell him.

'Where did you go?'

I point up at the crucifix.

'There. I went there.'

*

No one really understands where delusions come from, what they actually are. My feeling is that they are like waking dreams. My magpie mind gathers bits of experience about what I saw, thought, and felt during the day into my mind-nest, and weaves them with memories to create a story. When I am well, my mind plays these stories to me as dreams, and when I am unwell, they become delusions.

I see a crucifix on a wall in a bedroom and know that I'm going to sleep with this gruesome object watching over me. I have only slept in a room with a crucifix on the wall once before, in a monastery in Venice. So, perhaps my mind created a delusion that I was a monk to make sense of the strangeness of sleeping in a room with a crucifix. But why a gay monk?

A few years before we moved to Australia, Kai took me on an incredibly romantic and wonderful weekend in Venice. Apart from the fact that we both spent the whole weekend being worried that the other one was going to propose (female to male proposals run in both our families) and then being slightly disappointed that the other person hadn't. This weekend is in the top 10 holidays of my life.

Kai had booked us into a fantastic monastery on San Giorgio Maggiore, a small island overlooking St Mark's square. They generate a little extra money for candles and communion wafers by renting rooms to visitors. We were greeted at the huge wooden door by my first (and so far only) real-life monk, Brother Marcello. He was young and handsome, and, apart from the cassock, nothing like I'd imagined. He had a friendly smile, and when he looked at Kai, a softness came into his eyes.

We had put down our rucksacks in the cavernous entrance hall and the brother had led us into the plain kitchen and opened the fridge.

'Prosecco?' he asked in his softly accented English, gazing at Kai.

'No, *grazie*,' said Kai. 'I think we want to go and settle in.'

He got to his feet, and the brother sighed.

'Go. Go.' he said, waving his hand at us with a wry smile. 'Have fun!'

By the time we were safely in our bare room, with its thick whitewashed walls and its carved wooden crucifix, we were in floods of laughter.

'Do you think he fancied you?' I teased him, and we'd laughed again, barely registering the agonised Jesus looking down on us.

It had started raining, the stunning view across the lagoon blurred by sheets of water rushing from the clouds above. Thunder rumbled and lightning crackled and fizzed. We stood on the balcony under that shelter of an overhang to watch the storm, Kai's arm around my waist pulling me close.

CHAPTER 19

LOVE, LOVE IS A VERB. LOVE IS A DOING WORD.

Back in Sydney, under the gaze of a different carved Jesus, Kai is woken by our son's morning cry. The heavy medication holds me in a deep drugged sleep. It is Saturday, but I have an appointment with one of the GPs attached to the unit, so Kai shakes me awake. They are worried about my involuntary movements and want me to get a physical health check.

We file into the room and put our son in his buggy next to the seats. A round, middle-aged man with round glasses and a round stomach is sitting at the desk, a young Asian man beside him.

There is an examining couch in the corner. We take up the other two seats in the room.

'Hello, I'm Doctor Gill. I understand you've been having some difficulties?'

'Yes,' I reply, then look pointedly at the young man.

'This is a student who will be observing. You are okay with that?'

'No problem.'

There is a pause.

'So, tell me what's been going on with you physically. I've read your notes, so you don't need to worry about filling me in on your mental health. I'm here to help with what is going on physically.'

'I've been having some involuntary body movements. There are times when I don't feel in control of my body, which is scary enough, but it makes me very apprehensive about holding our son. I don't want to drop him.'

'Indeed.' He takes my hand and leans forward holding up an instrument. 'I'm just going to check your eyes,' he explains, shining a small light into my left eye. He flicks the light from one eye to the other while firing questions at me. I try to keep up with him.

'How old are you?'

'36.'

'What is your son's birthday?'

'28th January 2012.'

'Who is the Prime Minister?'

'Julia Gillard.'

'Where do you live?'

'Fairlight.'

'Where are you now?'

'St Jude the Good,' I fire back, and the doctor barks out a laugh.

'I think "St Anne Hospital" is the answer you're looking for.'

'Oh, shit,' I splutter as my right arm spasms.

He stops smiling and looks down at it. Then my left arm spasms, more violently, jerking my hand almost up to shoulder height. It is like I'm a puppet, my arms yanked by invisible strings.

'Oh, God,' I moan. 'What's happening to me?'

'Let's get you lying down.'

He takes my arm in a firm grip and leads me to the examining couch. A huge spasm ripples through my whole body and my knees give way. The doctor catches me, and Kai jumps up from his seat to take my other hand. They both lie me down on the couch.

'So frightened,' I whisper.

I have my eyes closed as one last spasm rips through me, and then it is over. Lying on my back, I stare up at the ceiling as I wait for my heart to slow down and my breathing to regulate.

'What do you know about Tourettes?'

'Tourettes?'

'Yes.'

'Swearing, I guess.'

'Anything else?'

'Do you think I have Tourettes?' I demand incredulously.

'No, I'm just trying to rule out certain conditions. I don't think you have Tourettes, or epilepsy. You remained conscious while you were having the involuntary movements. If you had epilepsy you wouldn't do that.'

'Good news, I suppose.'

I go to sit up, but the doctor stops me.

'Whoa there, Jennifer – just relax on your back for a minute.'

'Jen, call me Jen. So, what do you think it is, then?'

'It's most likely part of your mixed episode, part of your psychosis.'

Weird, I think, and I tell him so.

'Weird?'

'Well I was thinking about the mood stabilisers. It's a bit strange that I start taking an epilepsy drug and then start having fits.'

'Well, no, not fits. As I said, you'd need to be unconscious for us to consider epilepsy, so I can reassure you that you don't have that.'

I smile with relief, but the doubt remains. It just seems like too much of a coincidence. I wonder what they are trying to hide from me. *Why would they lie?* The paranoid thoughts swirl around me. Though I am much more in control, the delusional part of my mind is still trying to make connections where they don't exist. I close my eyes and rub the bridge of my nose with my hand.

'Sodium valproate is a very effective mood stabiliser. That is why you are taking it.'

I turn to smile at Kai. In the fluoro light of the small room, he looks pale and drawn with dark smudges under his eyes. But he smiles back at me.

'I feel a bit better now. I think I can get up.'

Those turn out to be the last of the involuntary body movements. I never find out why they happened or why they stopped. We also find out that some of the other patients and staff had vomiting, so it is extremely unlikely that my bout was part of my psychosis (though none of the staff acknowledge this).

One of the hard things about mental health problems is that they tend to overshadow physical problems. If you think you are Cameron Diaz, it is easy for other people to dismiss the things you are saying – that you have a terrible headache or backache, for example. This phenomenon is known as "diagnostic overshadowing", where the fact a person has a mental health diagnosis can cause GPs and other health professionals to focus less on the person's physical health.

My sister has struggled in the past to get some of her team of supporters to recognise her physical difficulties. Her last two relapses have been triggered by physical problems: a really bad toothache caused by years of neglect, and back pain caused by over-vigorous digging in her allotment. Both times, being in pain and needing someone around to help her brought home how alone she is, leading to feelings of sadness, and then to not taking her meds. Luckily, the current team looking after Jo really understand her and caught the bad-back relapse early. This meant she could go into a halfway house for intensive support rather than back to the psychiatric unit of the local hospital.

After the doctors, we head back to our room. I have a rest while Kai mixes a bottle and feeds my son on the wooden rocking chair, rocking backwards and forwards.

We have a canteen lunch of beer-battered fish and chips (skipping the salad this time), then we decide to explore some of the local area.

We discover Hornsby Park a few minutes' stroll away from the hospital. This beautiful green space is modelled on the Union Jack. The whole park is a rectangle with paths representing both the upright cross and the diagonal cross. In the centre of the two crosses, a large bandstand marks the middle of the park. Today, it is occupied by a trio of legging-clad women doing shoulder stands on their yoga mats.

As we stroll through in the afternoon sunshine, we watch an elegant pair of Chinese women doing the slow and controlled movement of Tai Chi. Footballs and frisbees are being kicked and thrown, and a group of Chinese or Korean men play a game that's played like volleyball but with a small, wicker ball. *This is the most beautiful park I've ever seen.*

We sit down on one of the benches overlooking the playing field.

'I've had two amazing ideas,' I announce.

'Yeah?'

'I'm going to set up a Hornsby Park Appreciation Society.'

'Sounds good.' Kai smiles at me.

'Also, I think the moon's gravitational pull affects our brains very slightly. I think this will be the key factor in finding a cure for schizophrenia – they always knew there was a link between the moon and madness, hence the word lunatic, "luna" meaning "moon".'

There is a pause, then he says, 'Interesting.'

'God, you are so sarcastic! You could just try to believe me.'

He bends his head forward and slowly rubs his face with his hands.

'I need a time out,' I snap. 'I'll take The Boy back to the hospital and you can stay here.'

'Okay.' His voice is flat, and he won't meet my eyes.

'I'm the one that's ill you know; you could try to be more considerate.'

Unbenknownst to me, Kai was starting to crack under the strain of seeing the one he loved so changed. During the next few days, he would walk to the park on his own and sit on a bench and just cry. His hope that a stay at Hornsby would make things better was wearing thin – I was still argumentative and highly irritable, especially if he didn't go along with my delusions. The arguments were very repetitive. The worst was when he felt I was attacking his personality, saying he was weak and not able to support me properly. It's still quite tough to have to come to terms with just how hard things were for him throughout this period.

Being so wrapped up in layers of mania and madness, I just don't see how much he's struggling and how selfish I'm being. Instead, I storm back, pushing the buggy quickly through the residential streets surrounding the hospital. When I get back, one of the nurses, Cathy, sees me push open the door to our room. She has large, doleful eyes, a puffed-up squashy face and short brown hair.

'Where have you been?'

'For a walk.'

'On your own?'

'Yes, for some of it.'

'You are not allowed out unescorted.'

I stare at her, stunned. Unescorted leave? *That is what my sister gets when she is in hospital but starting to gain more control.* But my situation is different; everyone keeps saying that – and this nurse is saying that *I'm* not allowed out on my own?

'What? No one told me! Why?'

'You are coming out of psychosis.'

'But I'm a voluntary patient, so how can I not be allowed out?'

'You can if you're escorted. It's just a safety precaution.'

*

My sister has spent years of her life in locked wards where she wasn't allowed out unescorted. She has been effectively locked up for years, against her will, in what is as close to prison as you can get without committing any crime, and with no idea how long her "sentence" is. When she is very ill, it's both the best and the worst place for her to be.

If you are paranoid and delusional, being watched all the time is very hard to take. And it doesn't help if your fellow inmates are just as unwell as (if not more so) than you.

A sane person locked up in a psych ward would shout and scream to be let out. All through her worst periods, Jo would think she was fine, and beg and plead to be freed.

The security is tight on locked wards. They often have an "airlock" system, with two sets of doors to get in and out. Before entering, you are given a locker in which to store forbidden items like matches or lighters. They open one door and you enter the airlock, then the first door is locked behind you before the second door opens.

Once she starts getting better, in any of the wards she's been on, Jo is given more and more freedom. The first time she was in hospital, she was there for 18 months, but after the first three, she had earnt their trust. It usually starts with her being escorted by two members of staff, then just one, then going out with family, and, finally, on her own.

One day, I was walking home from school after my GCSE maths exam and, for once, not thinking about my sister. I was planning the revision I would do that afternoon and thinking about the technology exam I had in two days' time.

When I got home and opened the gate, I saw my sister waiting on the front doorstep of our home. I stopped dead and stared up at her.

'I've come home,' she said. 'I don't want to be in hospital anymore.'

She sat leaning against the black-painted door, the brass knocker and figures one, zero and six above her head.

'Are you okay?' I asked.

'Hungry.'

I fished my keys out of the side pocket of my school bag and opened the door.

'Hello there!' called Helen, our cleaner. Helen came to the house every day to polish, iron, vacuum, and dust. She was also there so I had someone to come home to before Mum and Dad returned from work. (By this stage Tania had moved out of home, so it was just me, Jo, and Helen.)

'Hi, Helen, Jo's here,' I called up the stairs. There was a sudden silence as the vacuum cleaner was switched off. Then Helen came down the stairs. Jo walked past me and down into the kitchen, but I stayed in the hall, clutching my school bag as Helen walked towards me.

'You okay?' she asked furtively.

'I'll try to get hold of Mum,' I whispered.

She nodded and went into the kitchen, and I heard her cheery voice while she chatted to Jo. I raced up the stairs to the study and pulled the address book out of the shelf by the phone. I dialled Mum's direct line at Hackney College.

It rang through to voicemail.

'Mum, it's Jen. Jo's here – can you come home?'

I put down the phone and waited for a second, willing it to ring back and be Mum saying she would take care of everything. I searched through the address book to see if the main switchboard number was there. (Remember, this was before mobiles and Google!)

I tried again, but once more it went through to voicemail. A big sob gulped up from my stomach.

'Any luck?' asked Helen from where she was standing in the study doorway.

'No. Voicemail.'

She came in and put her hand on my shoulder. 'Don't worry, Jen – it'll be alright.'

'She attacked Mum last week.'

'Did she? I'm so sorry.'

'Grabbed her hair and dragged her to the ground.'

I tried the number again, and this time, Mum picked up.

'She's here. Jo's here.'

'Don't worry, I'll be straight home.'

'But what if she attacks you again?'

There was silence.

'It'll be okay, don't worry,' she said eventually. 'You sit tight, and I'll be back in 20 minutes.'

I hung up and slowly made my way down the stairs into the kitchen.

Jo had her back to me, but she turned when she heard me enter the room. She was holding a large knife in her right hand. The late afternoon light glinted on the blade. Her face was blank, and a hot flash of fear shot through me. *Was she going to stab me?* I stood still, looking at her, holding my breath. I tried a smile, but it was a pathetic attempt – too wide, too bright, with teeth showing.

A slow smile crept onto her face in return.

'Sandwich?' she asked, going back to the bread on the kitchen counter in front of her. She sawed back and forth through the crust and the soft middle of the loaf.

That moment right there, right there when I thought she might stab me, was one of the worst of my life. *She didn't want to stab me, she was just making a sandwich!* I felt the guilt soak through me. She had never – and has never – threatened me or shouted at me, not like she does sometimes with Mum and Dad. She always treated me well, even when she was really unwell.

'Jo, what are you doing here?'

She turned back to me, the bread forgotten for the moment.

'I want to come home. It's horrible in the hospital – I don't feel safe there. I'm not ill anymore, I'm better. I don't hear voices.'

'Hospital is the best place for you now.'

'That's just Mum talking, I know that. I know Mum doesn't want me back. That's because she is a vampire. That's why me and you are baby vampires.'

'Mum's not a vampire, Jo.'

She rolled her eyes and turned to the fridge. She took out butter, cheese, and ham, and placed them next to the sliced bread.

'Dad's a saint. You know that, right? He breathes for me.'

'When you say things like that, you don't sound better.'

She layered the cheese and ham onto the bread and flipped the second slice on top.

'I can't stay in hospital. It's so bad.'

'I know it's tough, but you're ill.'

'If I'm ill, then I should be with my family.'

I gave up and went to get a glass from the cupboard. I could hear a key scrabbling in the lock of the front door.

'I'm home!' called Mum.

Jo looked sharply towards the front door, her face contorted with hatred.

'Vampire,' she whispered, and I flinched. I was used to the anger and contempt that my sister had shown towards our parents from time to time since she was about 13, but this new level of hatred was terrifying to watch.

'I'll just clear up, shall I?' I said shakily, trying to lighten the situation. Stepping forward, I scooped up the knife and breadboard and put them in the sink, out of reach.

'I'm going to my room,' declared Jo as Mum entered the kitchen.

'Jo, I have to take you back,' she said firmly.

'I'm not going.'

'It's for the best.'

'What do you know?' Jo scoffed. She stomped downstairs to her room in the basement, her sandwich lying forgotten on the countertop.

Mum came over to me and held my hand.

'Are you okay?'

'Yeah, I'm fine. I was a bit ... ' I started crying. 'I thought she was going to stab me.'

Mum held me tight until my sobs lessened.

'Oh, Jen,' she sighed.

Now I'm a mother myself, I know that all my mum wanted to do was make things okay for me and for my sister, but in the face of the devastation of schizophrenia, there was almost nothing she could do for either of us. "It'll all be okay", the comforting words of a mother to a child, would have been a lie, and had no place with us on that day. It is a tough lesson to learn at 15, that things can go so wrong and stay wrong.

Mum, the brave woman that she is, managed to get Jo in the car and safely back to the ward. After they left, I went up to my room and looked at my technology folder. I sat at the desk, reading through my notes, failing in my efforts to memorise the definition of a nanofarad. The words on the paper were jumbled, jumping over each other. I leant forward and rested my forehead on the cool pages for a moment, but soon sat back up before the tears had a chance to drip onto the paper and smudge the words – I needed to be able to read them if I was going to get any revision done! I tried to focus, but it was hopeless. I spent a futile few hours not getting much done before I finally gave up.

*

Back at St Anne's, I'm starting to get a taste of what it must have been like for my sister over the years – but just a taste; here at St Anne Hospital, I have much more freedom than Jo. Yet still, the restrictions chafe.

We find out later that starting our stay at the beginning of a long weekend is less than ideal. Most of the senior people are away, and there is only a skeleton staff. This explains the curious lack of attention, even though I am being watched. No one comes to tell me what is going to happen, how things work, and what is expected of me. I later discover that they have a watch-and-wait brief with me.

I place my son in his pushchair next to me and stomp upstairs to get lunch. I am ravenous, and polish off a huge plate of chicken curry, rice, and poppadoms.

At this stage, along with all the other things they hadn't told us, they hadn't discussed the side-effects of the medication I was taking. I now know that olanzapine is well known for sedation and weight gain; it makes you very hungry. It may not be so serious, but weight gain can impact hugely on anyone's self-confidence, especially if you are already depressed and anxious.

But, as I didn't know this, I was eating for England.

I've always been able to eat whatever I want and not really put on weight (as long as I exercise), but the olanzapine dramatically alters my metabolism, as well as making me starving hungry. I put on five kilos in two weeks, adding to the extra five kilos I put on while I was pregnant. At first, I think my clothes have shrunk, I really do. As soon as they tell me about the side-effect, I'm able to stop eating so much, and my weight levels out.

After lunch, I find Kai lying on the bed with his eyes closed. I shut the door behind me.

'Now they are telling me I'm not allowed to go out on my own,' I complain.

'Jesus, this place ...' He covers his eyes with his arm.

'What are they going to do about it if I do? They can't fucking well watch me every moment! They won't even know I'm gone.'

He lets out a huge sigh.

'Sorry about earlier,' I murmur.

'S'okay. I'm just so tired.'

I sit next to him on the bed and put my hand on his arm. 'I just need you to believe me more.'

'But, Jen, some of the stuff you're saying is so *out there*. It's like when you thought that man was a paedophile; you knew it wasn't right the next day. I can't agree with stuff I know is wrong, can I? But you get so mad at me.'

We sit in silence.

'But what if I'm right and the moon … '

'No, Jen. No more.'

Later that afternoon I go into the patients' kitchen to sterilise my son's bottles. As I slosh the water around, thoughts about breastfeeding swirl around my head. I am still desperate to breastfeed. No one understands how much it matters to me – the staff just blithely assumed I would stop with no thought to the emotional repercussions. I feel like I've been robbed of the opportunity to do this one thing right. I've done so many other things "wrong": taking three types of medication during pregnancy, opting for a caesarean and not a "natural" birth … Sure, the doctor had recommended it, and mentioned the possibility of death to me during the decision-making process. And sure, secretly, I'd been relieved about that.

But not this.

I want to breastfeed, despite how much it hurts. I want to give my son the best, and I don't want people judging me for not breastfeeding. *Surely I won't be on the medication for long. As long as I continue to stimulate my breasts, I can go back to breastfeeding.*

No one explains that I'll need to keep taking the medication for months (if not years). I suppose it could have made me more upset to know that, and that's why they didn't tell me. Or maybe, as they knew I'd be on medication long-term, they just assumed I would somehow know this too. Or they all assumed someone else, someone more up to speed with my situation, would have explained it to me. Maybe they just didn't put that much thought into it, what with it seeming so obvious to an outsider that halting breastfeeding was the only sensible option.

Kai and I argue fiercely over breastfeeding. He tries to convince me that it is okay to stop, and I accuse him of not understanding how much it means to me. He finds out that, according to the Australian Breastfeeding Association, 92% of children are breastfed at birth, falling to 56% at three months, and only 14% at six months.

Looking back, I still don't understand why this was such a big deal for me as I genuinely believe that bottle-feeding is no problem. Some women, for many different reasons, just can't breastfeed.

I think it had something to do with control. Being a new mum and learning to care for a baby is a lesson in learning to live with chaos. There was so much in my life that was out of my control, especially being ill, I probably just wanted something to work the way it was "supposed" to.

The kitchen at St Anne's is small and neat, with rows of cabinets and a double sink along one wall, and a fridge and shelf with a row of sterilisers on the other. One of the other patients is feeding purée to her daughter, but she turns to greet me when I enter.

'Who is this little cutie?' I ask. The baby has short fair hair standing up in tufts around her head, and widely spaced, blue eyes.

'Rebecca. She's nine months old.'

'Wow, she's a good eater!'

Turning to the sterilisers, I open one to put in the bottles. I fill up the little reservoir with water and press the steaming button.

'I'm Patty.'

'Jen. Nice to meet you.'

'What are you in for?' she asks.

'That makes it sound like prison,' I laugh. Despite how annoyed I was getting at the staff, it was so far from my fears of being incarcerated. Nothing like the many horrible units I'd visited my sister in over the decades of her illness.

'But it is like prison here. I call us inmates rather than patients.'

'I've only just been admitted – I got here two days ago.'

'I've been here for weeks; this is my third stay.'

'I'm sorry to hear that.'

'I want to leave but they won't let me.'

Silence falls, and she turns back to her daughter, ladling spoonfuls of thick orange purée from a round Tupperware pot.

'What's that?' she says to her daughter. 'This is yummy, isn't it? I know you like this one. You're such a good girl. Yes, you are.'

She isn't doing anything that a thousand mothers haven't done when talking to their babies – holding a one-sided conversation. But there is something about the way she holds her head to one side, as if really listening, that reminds me of my sister, Jo.

When Jo was living in a hospital in Aylesbury, England, I went to visit her one weekend. We were having a café lunch in the market square when a man walked past with a little puppy on a lead. Jo loves dogs. Jo jumped up, leaving behind her egg and bacon sandwich and mug of tea, and ran over to the dog.

Crouching down next to it she said, 'Hello, you little thing. Aren't you cute?'

The owner smiled indulgently.

'Yes you are, yes you are.' She continued patting the little dog on its head. 'You're such a good dog. I know. I know.'

By now the owner was getting a little uncomfortable; Jo hadn't looked up at him or acknowledged him in any way.

I know that, on some level, Jo really thought the dog was communicating with her. It was not as extreme as hearing a voice, but was some way of "knowing" what the dog was thinking.

Just as I'm pretty sure, now, that Patty thinks her baby is really communicating with her.

'I have postpartum psychosis,' I say. 'That's what I'm in for.'

She turns to me. 'Me too.'

We both look at each other in silence. *Third visit*, I think, and my heart freezes. Will this happen to me? What if this isn't a short-term illness like the Extended Hours Team kept telling me?

Rebecca breaks the silence by calling for some more food with a soft burble.

Patty starts talking in a rapid stream, words tumbling out of her mouth as she tells me what has been happening to her. She is speaking so fast I can hardly keep up. I finish the bottles but don't know how to end the conversation.

'The second time I was admitted, she was six months, and I was in a terrible state. I thought that the government was spying on me. I know that they weren't, but they were at the same time, if that makes sense.'

In a strange way, it sort of does. I think back to my delusion that I was meeting Obama, and the walk I'd taken along the coastal path when I thought everyone around me was secret service, watching me, keeping me safe. It could just as easily have been a paranoid delusion that they were out to get me. And then there was the delusion that I had supressed a memory of childhood abuse. I saw her. She saw me.

'Nice to meet you. I've got to ...' I point at the door. She stops talking and wipes her daughter's sticky fingers with the kitchen sponge.

'See you in Group this afternoon?' she says as I leave the kitchen.

I run into one of the nurses, Olivia, on my way back to our room, and ask her about Group.

She brushes me off. 'Oh, we don't think you're ready for Group yet.'

'But what is it?'

'The patients come together and talk about their experiences with a facilitator. But you need to settle in a bit more first.'

'Another thing it would have been nice to know about,' I huff.

Olivia looks at me with her lips drawn together, then turns and walks back to the staffroom.

A bubble of irritation rises within me. Why can't they just explain what the fuck is going on? Can't they imagine, even for a moment, what it might actually be like to be a newly arrived patient in an actual psychiatric unit? This is their job, how they spend their time for a shift, but in between shifts, they get to go home, to relax, decompress, hang out with friends, do chores. This is my life now, and I have no control. Can't they picture how strange and confusing everything is for people like me?

CHAPTER 20

MAN, I CANNOT TAKE IT, IT'S ME OR IT'S THEM OR AM I GOING CRAZY?

The next day, Sunday, Kai stays in our room with The Boy while I go for an explore. In the middle of the confusing corridors, hallways, and rooms, I find a central courtyard. It has two large trees and mature plantings. It lies off a large wooden porch, which houses a small kiosk serving coffee and cakes. It is so peaceful, so calm. It was probably a courtyard when the building was a monastery. I think back to my monk delusions and imagine the monks coming to the courtyard for prayer and quiet meditation. I picture ghosts of figures tending to the plants and sitting on the old benches.

I sit and read my book under the porch. The friendly, chirpy young woman behind the counter greets and acknowledges the people who come to see her to fill up on coffee and cakes, tea and biscuits. When the queue dies down, she pulls out a chair at the table next to me and sits down for a second.

'What are you reading?' she asks, and we chit-chat about my book until another person comes to the kiosk for their coffee.

She is the first staff member I've spoken to who treats me just like an ordinary person, not a collection of vexing symptoms.

It is such a relief to just be a person buying a cup of tea, not an ill person. I smile as she bobs her dark head behind the coffee machine and we talk for a bit.

Suddenly, something catches my eye in the tree. It's an amazing bird – I've never seen anything like it before. It looks like half a bird, half a lizard. It has a long, fine neck and slim, rounded head. Its feathers are short, and they glisten like scales in the morning sunshine. I watch as it jumps from branch to branch, not realising that it's probably a delusion, like an augmented reality. There probably is a bird in the garden, but I doubt it looks quite like I think it does. I finish my tea and go back to the room.

'It's so nice in the courtyard,' I tell Kai.

'Yes, I went and had a coffee there yesterday when you said you wanted time out,' he tells me.

I can't keep on saying sorry, but I do.

'Sorry.'

'Jen, it's okay, but I do think it's a good idea for us to have some time apart. I can look after The Boy and you can have a break.'

'When do *you* get a break?'

He laughs.

'I'm not joking.'

'Jen, I–'

'Why do you always have to have the last word?'

'I don't. It's just–'

'See, you can't just leave it!'

'You asked me a question!'

'I know, and you just had to answer it!'

'What else could I do?'

'You just don't understand!'

'You're right. I really don't.'

'See, I told you.'

There is silence. He is looking at me, grief, annoyance, and concern layered through his face. I know he wants to say something – to have the last word. But then I realise that is the wrong way around. He always lets me have the last word. I don't realise that I was creating an argument out of nothing. Even now, I can remember how strongly I felt about "being right" and needing to prove that to him.

'I'll be back,' I say. 'They still haven't given me my meds this morning.'

I march out and go across to the staff room. As usual, the door is shut and the sign says "HANDOVER IN PROGRESS". I look through the glass. It doesn't look like a handover to me! Two nurses I don't recognise are chatting idly, while a third, Cathy, studies a manila folder of notes. They could even be my notes, for all I know. I hang around outside for a bit, trying to catch someone's eye, but no such luck. *This place is really starting to get to me*. In the end I knock loudly.

Cathy comes to the door.

'Yes?'

'My meds. I haven't had them yet.'

'Oh, yes – we were just about to come around.'

'I'm pretty sure I shouldn't have to remind you about my meds.'

The other two nurses in the room look up at the sharp tone of my voice. They look at my stony face and then one looks briefly at the other. I wonder if I'm starting to get a reputation for being difficult. *Well, good. If I am, maybe they will stop being so useless*.

'I assume it's a good idea to take them promptly at the same time each day? Or am I wrong?'

'No, you're right, but we were really just about to come around.'

She's just as bad as Kai, always having to have the last word. I can't help myself.

'Were you doing a handover?' I ask boldly.

'What?'

'It says so on the door.'

She looks at me with a wrinkled brow.

'Let's get your meds then, shall we?' she says with a bright, false smile.

Reaching back towards her desk, she picks up a bunch of keys and opens up the meds trolley. This is a small, desk-like piece of furniture on wheels. I stand next to her as she unlocks the top flap to reveal cubbyholes filled with white boxes with printed labels on them.

She gets out my meds and I take them. Just like that. *I wonder what they do with people who are resistant to taking their meds ...*

Back in the room, Kai is just settling my son down for a nap. I sit on the bed.

'This place is starting to get to me.'

He looks at me, trying to assess if he is "allowed" to reply.

'You and me both.'

*

Kai and I decide to set off for the local mall. The day before, when we were walking to the park, we'd noticed a swimming pool attached to the local private school.

'I wonder if I could go swimming there?' I'd said.

'Let's go in and see.'

We wandered in and found out that the pool isn't open to the public, but that I could come and have a swimming lesson if I liked.

'But I don't have my cossie here,' I'd complained to Kai.

'We could go to the mall and get you one.'

So now here I am, guiding the buggy out of our room and past the staff room to escape. I now know that I need to tell people if I'm going off-site, so I knock on the door despite the HANDOVER sign still being displayed.

'Just off to do a spot of shopping.'

'Are you going to the mall?' asks Cathy.

'Yes.' I prickle with annoyance. *Maybe this is another thing I'm not supposed to do.*

'I don't know if that's such a good idea. It's like a long, dark tunnel with people coming at you; all streaming out, all looking the same ...'

'Oh. Well, my husband will be with me so I'm sure it will be okay.'

And we leave.

As we walk through the park to the local Westfield, I tell Kai what Cathy said.

'Does make you wonder which one of you has mental health problems, if she thinks that,' he says, somewhat tongue-in-cheek. I grip his hand.

When we get to the mall, it doesn't remotely look like a long tunnel, but it is very busy. We decide to split up and meet again in two hours at the café in the mall entrance. I then go on the biggest spending spree of my life.

Normally, I hate shopping; I drag myself around the shops and have real difficulty buying something even if I really need it. But today, my normal hesitation disappears, and the wonders of the mall open up to me like a jewelled box of treasures.

I spend over $1,000 in one day. At Lorna Jane, I buy two pairs of yoga pants and a top, a box of socks, headband, two bikinis, and one sports bra. I chat to the sales assistant about Lorna Jane the person; she is so inspirational and makes clothes that are exactly what I want. I don't remember much of what she said, but I do remember her wide beaming smile becoming more and more fixed the longer I stayed in the shop. She showed me a book about Lorna Jane, which I also buy. I decide I am going to write another, much better, book about her, and her inspirational story.

I can barely contain my excitement at David Jones. I buy two expensive jumpers, a Country Road bag, a Ladybird notebook, and a pack of rainforest playing cards. At Diva, I buy three necklaces, five pairs of earrings, two rings and another headband. In a surf shop, I buy a bright blue wristwatch for $10. Bargain!

I enjoy the shopping like never before. It seems like a deeply meaningful activity. The things I buy are like missing parts of my soul. I feel like I can make myself whole again with these clothes, bags, and jewellery. It reminds me of the feeling I had as a child about a few items that I treasured, particularly a Brambly Hedge notebook and a strawberry scented eraser. I remember holding them and turning them over and over in my hands. I remember the strong feeling of contentment that I *owned* these perfect items.

I have the same absorbed attention with these new purchases: that they are somehow, mysteriously, enormously significant to me.

Overspending is a classic symptom of mania, and probably one of the many reasons that the nurses were reluctant to let me out unescorted; people with long-term or reoccurring mania can get themselves into serious debt.

I meet Kai at the appointed time, laden down with plastic bags full of treasure.

'I found so many good things – this mall is amazing!' I gush as we order (a skimmed flat white for Kai, English breakfast tea for me).

Kai looks at my pile of bags and says nothing, tucking the worry away with all the others. I didn't notice his uneasy expression;

I was on my first and only shopping high, and absolutely buzzing with excitement.

Luckily, we'd saved up a fair amount to cope with going down to one salary while I was on maternity leave, so the spending doesn't put us into the red.

*

After my shopping success, we head back to the hospital. I'd noticed a sign for art therapy, so, after a lunch of beef casserole and mash, I leave Kai with my son and head for the appointed room.

I find it through two dark double doors at the end of a long, upward-slanting corridor.

There are two people waiting to go in: one woman with straight black hair and huge dark eyes, and the square man with square glasses whom I'd seen in the dining room on our first day in hospital.

'Hello,' I say to the woman. 'Is this for art therapy?'

'Yes. Your first time?'

'Yep.'

'Well, you're in for a treat.' She smiles at me.

By the time the two staff members arrive, there are 10 or so people waiting, either leaning against the wall or sitting on the floor of the corridor outside the room. One of them opens the door and we file inside.

The room is amazing! It has one wall of storage, with drawings and paintings stuck to the doors of the cupboards. The art is a riot of colour and textures. One catches my eye – a picture of a brain with arrows pointing. Words on the page say, 'Art is a way for the brain to heal itself.'

After moving to Australia, the light and beauty of where we lived gave me the inspiration to explore my artistic side, something I hadn't done since secondary school. And I had more free time than when I lived in London. I did a photography evening course and spent happy afternoons going on solo photography expeditions with my new SLR camera, a birthday present from Kai. My friend taught me how to do lino cuts. I bought myself a large expensive sketch book and I made collages out of maps and other found material.

But I haven't experienced anything like this before. The room hums with energy and everyone is vibrating too.

The counter, which runs around two sides of the room, is full of boxes with every type of art material you can imagine. There are palettes and tubes of paint; and boxes and boxes of coloured pencils, charcoal, and chalk; and miniature chests of drawers filled with beads and jewellery-making materials. I feel all the materials calling out to me.

We all cluster around a table in the middle of the room. A young woman opposite me gets out a half-finished drawing. It is of a phoenix rising from flames that seem to flicker and dance on the page.

'That's good.' I compliment her work. She smiles, nods, and goes back to drawing the flames in orange pencil.

A clean sheet of paper is calling out particularly strongly, so I carefully pick it up and place it on the table in front of my seat. It is so clean, white, and unblemished that it seems almost criminal to mark its virginal beauty. My hand hovers over a pencil jar filled with markers, crayons, and pencils. They are vibrating at different frequencies. One, however, is still among the humming, whirling mass, and I carefully slide it out of the jar. It is a blue marker pen with a thick nib. It's like the pen is signalling to me that I must pick it. I don't know why.

I start to draw. Sweeps and curls of blue fill the paper in front of me. I pick up a handful of plaster of Paris shells from a container on the counter behind me and hunt down some glue.

As I am sticking the shells to the paper, I notice the woman with the dark eyes is quietly crying. As I look at her, the room shifts slightly and stops humming.

She and the woman next to her are making jewellery. She is holding a thin metal loop and stringing beads onto it as the tears roll down her face.

'I miss them so much,' she sobs.

Her friend is sitting quietly by her side looking at the beads she has collected in front of her. I look around, but the two staff members are engrossed with two other patients and their art. Instead, I slink over to one of the art therapists. She looks up at me with her eyebrows raised.

'Do you have any tissues?' I whisper, motioning towards the crying woman.

'Yes, of course,' she says handing them to me. To my surprise she doesn't go over to the tearful woman herself.

Sitting back down, I hand the tissue box to the woman. Her friend flashes a grateful smile.

'Are you okay?' I ask.

'I thought I was going home today. But they tell me I can't.'

'I'm sorry.'

'It's my daughter's birthday tomorrow and I thought I'd be out of here. I'm making this for her.'

She holds up the small bracelet.

'How old?'

'Nine. And my eldest is eleven.'

There is a pause. She looks at my drawing.

'I like that.' She smiles at me through her tears.

I carry on creating swirls and loops, thinking about my illness and how long it might last. *Will I still need medication, or hospital, when my son is nine?* The thought chills me. I look down at my drawing and start to panic.

The walls seem suddenly to loom inwards with their claustrophobic piles of clutter. I start to get to my feet when one of the art therapists sits down next to me.

'I like this,' she says.

'Oh, thanks. They're sort of doodles, really.'

'I like your mix of materials: paper, pen, and plaster of Paris. Very creative.'

I smile shyly at her. The feeling of panic is fading a little.

The hour draws to a close and we all start packing up our art. Pencils and chalk go back into the cluster of pencil boxes in the middle of the table. The man with square glasses turns the canvas he's been working on to show one of the staff members. It's an abstract landscape with an orange swirl for a sun and twisted, purple gum trees.

'You've managed to capture the calm before the thunderstorm.' The therapist praises him.

He smiles and props the canvas on the counter to dry.

Since I've done my packing away, I get up to go back to Kai and The Boy.

'I hope you get to leave soon,' I say to the dark-eyed woman as I duck out the door.

Once again, dinnertime passes without the nurses giving me my meds. Last night we'd tried an experiment to see if they would totally forget if we didn't nag them. They did eventually come with a handful of tablets, but I'd already fallen asleep and Kai had to wake me up. In a way, we were getting used to this slackness. But in hindsight, it didn't fit any model of best practice care – and it loomed large for me because of my elevated levels of irritation. I felt as if I was being "done to" rather than "co-operated with".

I go to the staff room. As usual the door is shut and the "HANDOVER IN PROGRESS" sign is up. This time, I don't wait around to see if I can catch someone's eye and just knock straightaway. Olivia comes to the door.

'Meds?'

'Oh, yes – give me a minute.'

She grabs her keys from the desk and steps to the medication cabinet in the corridor. She flips open the doors and starts riffling through the boxes of medication.

'Right, so what do we need for you?' she asks.

'Don't you know? It should be on my notes.'

She sighs. 'Yes, it will be in your notes, but it's a good idea if you also know what medication you are taking.'

'I don't know it off by heart, but I have it written down. I could get my notebook?'

'No, that's fine; I'll just check your notes.'

She goes back into the staffroom to get my notes and then comes back and picks up three boxes from the cabinet. She pops pills out of blister packs and hands them to me in a small paper cup.

'Why do I have to keep reminding you about my meds?'

Olivia sighs again.

'It is just, if I wasn't being compliant, I'd be missing my meds, wouldn't I?'

'We shouldn't have to remind you,' she retorts.

She is being impossible. Always having to have the last word. Just like Kai earlier. Why does everyone want to argue with me?

'Well, I feel I shouldn't *have* to remind you!'

'There you go,' she says.

'Oh, and by the way, was a handover in progress?'

'What?'

'Well, the sign on the door says "HANDOVER IN PROGRESS", but it's always up.'

'Jen, how are you feeling?'

'I'm fine, really; just getting frustrated with how things are run here.'

'You just need to give it time. Things will come right in a few days when the medication has had a chance to kick in properly.'

She looks at me with concern in her eyes. She can't accept that I might have legitimate reasons to complain. She sees me only as a woman with a mental health problem, and not as someone who might have real reasons to be annoyed. I felt overwhelmed with hopeless rage. There was nothing I could do, I had no power. I let her have the last word and wonder what observation about my state of mind she might record on my notes. Perhaps, "Jen is highly irritable and resisting taking ownership of her medication".

The next morning, Monday, we are walking out of the ward to go to my swimming lesson. I have a bag packed with a brand-new bikini, towel, and goggles. We walk past Cathy in the corridor.

'Where are you going?' she asks, frowning.

'Swimming,' I say.

'We need you to do a blood test. Can you go later?'

'But I have a swimming lesson booked!'

'A lesson?!'

I can see in her face that this is yet another "mad" thing – proof that I'm not in my right mind.

'But you need the blood test,' she protests.

'No one told me about a bloody blood test. Why do you keep springing these things on me? What do I need a blood test for, anyway?'

She purses her lips and looks at the clock. 'To measure the sodium valproate levels to make sure the dose is correct.'

I take a deep breath and try to calm down.

'I'll be back by eleven – would that work?' I offer, trying to be reasonable.

'Well now's more convenient ... '

'Not for me, it's not.'

Kai takes charge. 'Come on, Jen,' he says, then turns to Cathy. 'We'll do the blood test later. You'll just have to fit it in.'

He takes my hand and we sweep down the corridor.

'Thanks, babes. I'm really getting to the end of my tether with this place.'

'Me too.'

In the large glass foyer of the swimming pool, a woman in her mid-fifties is waiting at the reception desk. She has short dark hair and a swimmer's broad shoulders. She smiles at me expectantly.

'I've come for my lesson,' I say.

'That's me. Come downstairs and we'll get going.'

I strip off my clothes by the side of the empty pool. Kai sits with my son asleep in the buggy and reads emails on his phone.

'Do you have anything specific you'd like to focus on?'

'Front crawl. I only breathe on one side and I'd like to be able to breathe on both sides. You don't call it "crawl" though; freestyle, I think.'

'Yes. I've never understood why you Poms call it "crawl",' she says.

I jump into the water, a sense of calm settling over me as it closes over my head. I stand up, the water running over my head and shoulders.

'Right, so let's do two lengths to warm up,' the instructor declares.

By the end of the lesson, I have learnt bilateral breathing and I am out of breath, my heart pumping.

Physical exercise is recommended to everyone to improve physical health, and it's even more beneficial when you have mental health problems. The natural endorphins that kick in when you have finished your run or yoga session can counterbalance feelings of sadness or anxiety. It's almost as if your mind and your body are one, and what benefits one, will benefit the other. Most people feel better when they get regular physical exercise – something the staff at St Anne's should note.

My sister has had dramatic weight fluctuations over the years. She was a slender size 10 before she became ill, but years of heavy medication, boredom, and no opportunity to exercise have taken their toll, and now she's more like a size 16 or 18.

Paradoxically, her weight can be an indication of how well she is; when she slims down, we know it's because she hasn't been taking her meds. Now that she's committed to taking her medication, however, she's larger. She doesn't seem to let it bother her, though – a small price to pay for sanity, some might think.

Later, as I battle to lose the weight I put on during that time, I wish someone had explained the possible side-effects to me in more detail. I had no idea about any side-effects, weight gain just being the most obvious.

*

We make our way back to the hospital and let the staff know that we can do the blood test any time. Cathy shows in a slim Indian woman. She is carrying a large tool-box-shaped container which she plonks on the bed. I give her a huge smile and ask her how she is. She returns it shyly as she snaps open the fasteners and lifts out a needle and blood-collecting tube.

'Very cute,' she says nodding at my son, who is having a cuddle with Kai in the rocking chair.

'Thank you, we think so too.'

She gets me to sit down on the edge of the bed and roll up my sleeve. There is the faint smell of chlorine as I haven't had a chance to have a shower since my swim. She coos at the baby as she finds a vein, then concentrates on my arm as she inserts the needle.

'Okay?' she asks.

'Yes, fine.'

After she leaves, I jump in the shower and wash off the chlorine. Then we go to get yet another canteen lunch.

That afternoon, my good friend, Holly, comes to visit, driving from Terrey Hills to Hornsby. We sit in the courtyard and sip coffee (her) and tea (me). I tell her a bit of what has been happening.

'It has been really frightening but I feel so much better now.'

'Psychosis, psyshmosis,' she says. 'You seem fine to me.'

And I am fine at that moment.

One of the hardest things for Kai was that I would be fine for long stretches, but then, with no warning, I would suddenly become really argumentative. Most days he would go to Hornsby Park and sit and cry. It breaks my heart to think of him there, alone and sad, because I had raged and ranted about something that I wouldn't even remember the next day. Mental illness takes a heavy toll on loved ones – something I have vivid first-hand experience of – but let me tell you, I now know that it's nothing compared to the pain and extreme confusion of experiencing mental illness yourself.

When my sister was first in hospital in Homerton, I tried to visit her often (though not as often as I should have). I would roll up my trousers and tuck them into my socks, clip on my bicycle helmet, carry the bike up the stairs from the basement, and pedal to the hospital via Hackney Downs and the Chatsworth Road.

I remember the feeling of dread – partly of seeing my beautiful, fun-loving sister so frightened and confused, and partly of seeing the other patients. On one visit we were in the TV room with one of her new friends from the ward. The room was square with high ceilings. The curtains were drawn, and it was gloomy and dark. The TV was bolted at the top of one wall in a corner. There were two young men watching the TV, and one man sitting at one of the other tables, slowly flicking through a pack of playing cards.

There was a soft snapping sound as he turned over each card amid the burbling of the TV in the background.

He had a shaved head and light-brown skin. His scalp was rippled and folded as if his skull had melted into his brain. I wanted to bundle my sister up and take her away from that place, and from that man. I wanted to make her safe. But most of all, I wanted her not to have been ill.

But I don't remember Jo ever saying she was scared.

'Marcel is a good friend,' she said. 'One of the few good people here.'

Marcel looked at me with his dull brown eyes and smiled, but I couldn't meet his dead stare. I now realise that it would have been kinder not to judge him from his appearance but I'm going to let 15-year-old me off that one.

CHAPTER 21

I ALWAYS FEEL LIKE SOMEBODY'S WATCHING ME

The days pass with meals in the canteen, walks in the park, and sessions with Toby, the registrar psychiatrist. My mania was still strong in the first few days – hence all the arguments with Kai – but had almost completely gone by the end of my stay, thanks to the fast-acting antipsychotic medication. Kai and I slowly start to get back to our normal, wonderful relationship, defined by kindness, care, and understanding – not snap judgements and harsh words. It is a huge relief that my periods of extreme irritation become few and far between as the days tick by, though we do get steadily more and more irritated by the staff. We come to realise that the best place for me to get better is at home among my familiar things, and not being scrutinised, all hours of the day, by the various staff members.

We try to express our dissatisfaction, and they do try to listen, but I have the very strong feeling they are discounting my difficulties as being part of my illness rather than anything that they are doing wrong. They find it harder to brush off Kai, who starts having to be very assertive and advocate for me. Eventually, they have no choice but to listen to us. I find it incredibly frustrating that they will listen to my husband and not to me, but I'm so glad he's there – it proves that my annoyance is "real" if he's annoyed too.

One of the hardest things about having a serious mental illness is that your own thoughts and feelings are often dismissed and brushed off as a part of your illness rather than being valid thoughts and feelings.

Over the years, my sister has had many run-ins with the staff who have been looking after her. There was one horrible incident when she was being driven to her flat by one of the psychiatric nurses while on escorted leave. She was taken by the conviction that this nurse was going to harm her, and, at a set of traffic lights, she burst open the door, climbed onto the bonnet and started trying to rip off the windscreen wipers. She wasn't given leave for a little while after that.

In another secure ward, one of the highest security ones she has ever stayed in, they wouldn't even let her have a cup of tea if there was someone else in the room in case she threw it. One day, she managed to smuggle rocks in from the patch of garden in which they were allowed, and threw them at the glass of the central nurses' station. All the staff stood open-mouthed as she raged at them. Luckily, the glass was toughened and no one was hurt.

Now that I myself am subject to the power and control the staff have over me (even as a voluntary patient), I understand her frustration and anger. I sometimes feel like throwing a few stones myself and ripping that "HANDOVER IN PROGRESS" sign into little pieces.

It fills me with sadness that, whether she was right or wrong in her feelings towards the staff, Jo didn't have anyone with her to advocate for her as I do with Kai. My parents have tried, but this hasn't always been easy due to Jo's paranoia. The most awful thing is that, even if the things she thought the staff were doing to her were delusions, she would have experienced them as real.

And the feeling that no one believed her must have been awful to bear in the midst of her muddled and paranoid thinking. One of the silver linings of my own experience of psychosis is that it has given me a greater understanding of my sister's experience. It hasn't made her difficult, erratic behaviour any easier to deal with – it is still difficult and erratic, after all! But when I spend time with her, I can remember how it felt.

*

On Thursday, we are walking in the park. The sun is warm, and the noisy myna birds are calling to each other from the large trees dotted throughout the park. I'm pushing the buggy and Kai is holding my hand. The Boy is burbling away, waving his hands and feet in the air.

'I think the worst is over,' I announce.

'Me too,' he says. He gives me a tight hug.

'I'm feeling much more like myself.'

'I can tell.'

And the worst *is* over. For the time being, anyway.

The afternoon passes in a glow of peace and contentment, the happiness of which I'm still feeling that night. We settle my son, have dinner, and tuck ourselves into the double bed.

'Even though this place is getting to us, we are actually really lucky that you got a place here,' says Kai. 'Imagine if you'd had to go into hospital without me or The Boy.'

'Don't. Even though we're getting sick of the staff, it's not been as bad as I feared; nothing like any of the hospitals Jo's been in. But, as everyone keeps telling me, I am different to my sister.'

He rolls over and we press our bodies tightly together. We have a soft, warm kiss.

One thing is just about to lead to another when the door creaks open and an upside-down L of light streams into the room around the door. A figure is outlined against the bright light of the corridor. She is carrying a torch.

Kai jumps up and we both clamp the duvet over our nakedness.

'Who's that?' I ask sharply.

'Just me – Magda.'

'What are you doing? It's eleven o'clock!'

'I'm just doing obs.'

'What the hell is that?'

'Jen,' warns Kai. I can hear the tension in his voice.

'Well, we need to keep an eye on you.' She shrugs and closes the door.

'For fuck's sake,' I huff. 'She didn't even knock.'

'What timing. Thank God we weren't, you know, at it!'

We burst out laughing, and the tension diffuses a little.

'Well, we're going to have to sleep with PJs on now. No more Mr Naked Guy,' says Kai.

CHAPTER 22

JUST HOLD ON, WE'RE GOING HOME

The next morning, we ask Olivia what obs are.

'Observations. You're just coming out of psychosis, so we need to monitor you.'

'Even when we are asleep?'

'You might not be asleep, that's the point.'

'How often do you check?'

'Every hour.'

'*What?!* Why didn't anyone tell us?'

I stare at her, open-mouthed. I am stunned. *Every hour?* No wonder I feel uneasy here, being "observed" in this way! That line from *Catch 22* comes to me, 'Just because you're paranoid doesn't mean they aren't after you.' (When I say "comes to me", I vaguely remember someone saying something about it, and me scribbling it down on my increasingly long shit-I-need-to-try-and-figure-out-when-my-mind-stops-fucking-with-me list.)

I appreciate that it's the staff's way of managing the risk of my illness, but holy cow, imagine if everyone was watching you so closely while you tried to learn how to parent a small baby and were feeling so completely weird!

'Last night someone walked in on us almost having sex.'

One of the other patients is walking past just as I say this. She is a tall woman with long dark hair parted in the middle. She has a long skirt and bare feet. She stops to lean against the wall just outside the staff room.

'Oh, dear.' Olivia falters, looking concerned.

I wonder if wanting to have sex in the middle of a crisis is another "symptom" of my psychosis, just like the vomiting and involuntary body movements. It's almost as if anything that happens to me will be attributed to the psychosis. I felt hopeless, my illness pinned over the real me, being judged and watched and assessed through the lens of mental illness overshadowing everything else about me.

'It would have been nice if someone had told us, warned us! It's yet another thing that we haven't been told about. Just because I'm unwell and a patient here, it doesn't mean we're not entitled to our privacy!'

'Come on, Jen, let's get breakfast,' says Kai hurriedly, taking my hand and leading me away. We walk past the tall woman.

'I hear what you're saying,' she whispers to me.

At breakfast, we talk plans.

'I want to leave,' I state.

'I agree. The best place for you is at home – it's doing you no good being scrutinised all day long.'

His ready agreement surprises me, but I think he can see how agitated I'm getting with the constraints of the hospital and the attitude of the staff. He knows me better than anyone and can see that the delusional stage has all but passed.

'We have a meeting with Toby this morning, don't we? We can tell him then.'

*

'We want to leave,' I say to Toby later that morning when we're sitting in his little rectangular office.

'Can you tell me why?'

'We think the best place for me to be is at home. We are getting quite annoyed at the way the staff are treating us – well, me, really.'

Kai nods.

'Why?' asks Toby.

'Well, lots of things. I have to keep reminding them to give me meds. The handover sign is always up and the door closed – or at least, it seems that way to us. If someone had just taken the time to explain how things work in the first place, it wouldn't have been so bad. But we seem to find things out by accident. There is a Group that no one told us about. And the fact that I'm not allowed out on my own, which doesn't make sense when I'm a voluntary patient. And obs. Someone actually walked in on us nearly having sex last night.'

Toby laughs nervously.

'Have you been warned about the side-effect of mood stabilisers?'

'No, I don't think so.'

'It can cause severe birth defects if you take it while pregnant, so you need to make sure you are taking precautions.'

'Surely someone should have told us that, and about any other side-effects. I'm not planning to get pregnant any time soon – or ever again, for that matter – but what if we were considering it? That's another really good example of what we're finding difficult here. It's almost like everyone is assuming someone else has filled us in.'

'I see.'

'Also, I feel like I'm being treated as a collection of symptoms, not a person. It seems like everything that happens, or that I do, is put down to my psychosis.'

'Like what?'

'I was throwing up on my first night and the nurse said it was linked to my psychosis, and then we found out that a few other people had been sick, so it was probably a bug or food poisoning. It's like they just discount anything I say because I'm mentally ill. It is a horrible, belittling feeling of being ignored, being dismissed.'

'I see,' he says again.

'But the worst thing is the feeling of being scrutinised the whole time. Like right now, I'm talking to you, but I know you are observing me and looking for signs of the state of my mental health. It sounds a bit paranoid, I know, but you're not paranoid if everyone is actually looking at you the whole time.'

He laughs. 'Yes, I can see how that would be quite off-putting.'

'It is more than off-putting! It is very, very difficult to deal with when I am feeling so vulnerable.'

He nods.

'Though I'm feeling so much better,' I quickly add. 'I just want to go home and start learning how to be a mum again.'

Being judged and scrutinised, and constantly feeling dismissed because everything is "part of your illness" when you're already in turmoil puts a massive hole in your self-confidence. When you're a new mum, you're learning on the hop how to deal with a million and one new situations. One of the bits of advice you hear is to try to trust your instincts. At this stage, I just want to go home and try to get to grips with life again.

'I'm sorry you've been having a not-great experience. We really would recommend you stay. But you're right, you are a voluntary patient so you're free to leave. If you can wait till this afternoon, I'd like you to meet Professor Metcalf who is in charge around here.'

'Another meeting with people staring at me.'

'Well, we'll try not to stare.' He tries a weak smile on me.

I look at Kai and he nods.

'Okay, we'll wait until then, but we are determined to go.'

The meeting with Professor Metcalf is scheduled for two o'clock, so we go back to the room and start packing up. At five to two, we file back into the little office. My son starts to cry, so Kai picks him up to comfort him.

Toby introduces us to Professor Metcalf and a third member of staff, Heather, who is in charge of the nurses. She has been on holiday, she explains.

'But I'm back now, and want to make sure we improve things for you.'

Professor Metcalf is a tall, slim woman with a prominent nose and brown wavy hair. She is wearing a trouser suit in a soft grey material. She has a necklace of large green beads resting on her shirt.

'I hear that you have been having difficulties and want to leave,' says Professor Metcalf. 'This is why we asked Heather to sit in on this meeting, so she can hear some of the problems you've been having and see if there is anything we can do to make things better.'

'We really are keen to go,' I say to her and repeat what we said earlier to Toby.

She listens carefully with a grave face. As I talk, I feel the eyes of everyone in the room boring into me, Professor Metcalf, Toby, Heather, and even Kai's. I rub my face with one hand.

'I understand that you need to keep an eye on us patients, but it's the scrutiny that is just getting too much to bear. Toby says you'd prefer for me to stay but I can leave if I want. So we are going to leave.'

'I understand, but I must just say again that we think it is too soon for you to leave.'

'But I'm feeling much better.'

How many times had I heard Jo say this when she was still seriously ill and desperate to get out of hospital? I feel a sob welling up. I try to clamp it down. It is vital that I don't cry in front of Professor Metcalf. A voice inside me whispers, *'Crying is weakness. If I cry, they will think I can't cope.'*

'You've only just come out of psychosis! You are still in the middle of your mixed episode.'

'What's that? I thought I had postpartum psychosis?'

'It is more accurate to say "mixed episode" as you've also experienced mania and grandiose thinking, as well as delusions and hallucinations.'

'I haven't had any delusions since the first day, or any involuntary body movements! I think I'm almost back to normal.'

I smile at all three of them, but their eyes continue to bore into me. I feel trapped by their collective gaze like an insect in amber. I feel the sob again, fighting to get out of my chest.

I believed this to be true at the time. I'd thought that my monk delusion was the last one, but now I realise I was still far from well. Even seeing the lizard bird in the courtyard had been a delusion. I was definitely still somewhat manic, still occasionally arguing with Kai and having strange thoughts.

But we do leave that day. And we do manage to cope for a few weeks. Until the next thing to go wrong, goes wrong.

CHAPTER 23

BACK TO LIFE. BACK TO REALITY.

Jo has had many delusions over the years. Many were paranoid, like when she thought Mum was a vampire wanting to hurt her, and some were dangerous, like when she thought she could fly and tried to jump out of a window. All of them were confusing.

A few years ago, I was visiting her in a high-security unit (the one where she threw the stones). She really was very unwell; one of the worst periods she'd had. We sat in the visitors' room, facing each other on institutional armchairs next to the institutional pine coffee table.

She was jumpy and distracted.

'How are you doing, Jo?' I asked.

'Okay, but–'

And then she stopped, staring out through the window. A look of alarm bloomed on her face. All of a sudden, she jumped to her feet with a sharp intake of breath.

'The princes! They're in danger!'

'Which princes?'

'William and Harry – they're in terrible danger!'

'No, Jo, I don't think so. I think they have lots of bodyguards.'

I got up and held out my hand. She took it and I gave her hand a squeeze.

'Come and sit back down, Jo. Everything is okay.'

She moved back to her chair and we both sat back down, although she was looking nervously around the room.

'Are you sure?'

'Yes. So, tell me about the art you've been doing ...'

She smiled at me and the delusion was forgotten.

One of the things I have learnt from my experience is that, no matter how wild or crazy it sounds, when you are having the delusion, it feels like reality. So, even though I'd seen my sister struggle to control her own delusions, it didn't help me in the moments when I was gripped by delusion. It takes a lot of insight into your own illness to realise that you are having a delusion while you are having it. Jo, partly due to the years she has had to bear her illness, does sometimes have this insight and you can talk her down, but only sometimes.

Kai has also learnt this over the last few weeks, but still wants me to come home.

As we drive back to Fairlight with the car packed and my son safely in his car seat, I realise this is an ending of sorts. I also realise some truths about what has happened to me.

And the truth is this:

- Renée Zellweger isn't living in my building, and she hasn't had a child
- I'm not Cameron Diaz
- Peter isn't a millionaire married to Lindsay Lohan
- I'm not going to cure cerebral palsy
- Or schizophrenia
- Or catch all paedophiles
- I didn't travel back in time to be the first human ever

I have to let go of all these experiences that felt so real at the time but which I now know are delusions. All apart from one – that I am going to write a book. You are holding it in your hands right now. I can't tell you how good it feels to have gone and done it, actually written a book and got someone to publish it!

Since leaving, I've thought a lot about why the hospital didn't work for us. This is what I wish I'd said to Professor Metcalf and the other staff in that last meeting:

'It is disconcerting, to say the least, to be treated as mentally ill first and a person second. I felt like a cluster of symptoms held together in the meat sack that is my body. Mind, body, and spirit is the whole of me. I know part of my irritation and unreasonableness was due to my illness, but not all of it. I don't want you to dismiss all I am saying because I was still gripped (especially in the first few days) by mania and delusions. I know at least some of what I felt is real. Also, as Kai was also getting very annoyed, and he wasn't ill, I hope you will be able to really listen to what I have to say.

'While this unit is cutting-edge in terms of not splitting up mothers and their babies, it still has a way to go in really treating patients as people first. You need some sort of induction (or even a welcome pack) to the unit, to explain how things work and what is expected of patients and what they can expect from the staff. It would work really well if each patient had a "main carer", someone who is that patient's main support, to avoid the problem of staff assuming someone else has filled us in on important matters, or explained what is going on. I know you attempted to assign me with a main point of contact, but the following day she wasn't in, and no one stepped in to take her place.

'I also felt powerless, even as a voluntary patient, and it felt like I would be "punished" for complaining or be labelled as "a difficult patient". More care and support should have been made available to help me let go of the idea that I must breastfeed. It felt like it wasn't important enough to register with the staff. It was really important to me. It felt like the staff where there for crisis, not ongoing care.

'The staff should remind themselves every day, though the situation is work for them, it is everything to the patients. Our whole lives have reached this dreadful crisis point, when we thought we'd be cooing over a lovely new baby. I know my fear of going mad and getting sectioned was much stronger than most, but I think any woman would be extremely distressed and unhappy that things had gone so badly wrong. You should hold the thought that the illness isn't all that makes up patients' lives, and work in a way that helps build up our self-confidence, which has taken a severe hammering. You should encourage your patients to be active, not discourage them. Most of all, you need to take down that bloody handover sign.'

That's what I should have said.

*

When we open the door to our apartment and pile the bags up by the door, I feel a huge weight lift from my shoulders. The water outside is a sheet of gunmetal grey with kinks of silver where the wind is ruffling its surface. I sit down in the brown leather IKEA rocking chair and close my eyes.

'Good to be home?' asks Kai.

'Like you wouldn't believe,' I reply. He moves over to me and gently places my son in my arms.

'Here, I'll start unpacking.'

I hug my son tight, and when he starts to wiggle, I lay out the beautiful knitted blanket that my friend Hilary made on the floor and lay him down on it. I can hear Kai moving around the bedroom, methodically emptying the bags and piling clothes into the wash basket.

Now I can just focus on getting back to normal.

'Not yet, not yet,' the Gods of Fate or Chance whisper above me.

I still have one more ordeal to face up to and survive.

Postnatal depression.

PART II

CHAPTER 24

I WILL LET YOU DOWN, I WILL MAKE YOU HURT

Wherever I go, there I am.

My diary entry.

This is the shortest part of the book, though it covers the longest period. Why? Because the depression, when it came crashing over me, squeezing out all joy, all happiness, all light, left behind days upon days, weeks upon weeks of ground-hog-day-like repetition.

The grinding awfulness of each long, long day was only made worse by the mind-numbing boredom; my concentration was shot, making it hard to read – even a magazine was too much for me. But boredom is way too weak a word to describe how I felt. It was how I imagine being in a war feels: the mix of terror, fear, and long periods where nothing much happens but you still have to be on your guard, never able to relax.

*

I've been out of hospital for a week and a half when the depression comes. I've been coping quite well with Kai back at work; I've managed to get out and about, meeting up with women from the mothers' group and my other friends with small children.

On the first day of my depression I go to the gym – our local Fitness First. I'd joined the week before and, in hindsight, I probably was still a bit manic – I thought it was all going to be wonderful and that I'd get back into shape in no time. They have a crèche there called Playzone, which gives you an hour and a half of childminding for less than $6. It is my second time using Playzone, and I go to a body pump class and then have a long, relaxed shower after my workout. It feels amazingly luxurious.

By the time I go to pick up my son, with just minutes to spare before they shut for the day, he is beside himself, crying and crying. They haven't been able to get him to sleep, and once he misses his first sleep, he misses his second, and only sleeps for 30 minutes for his third. He is a crying, complaining baby for the whole day, which is so unlike his usual chilled-baby status. I go from being fine (if a bit anxious) to getting more and more upset as the day and his crying continues on and on.

I'm desperate by the end of the afternoon, totally defeated by the continuous crying. I know some women have babies who cry a lot most days, and my heart goes out to them; I could barely cope with just one day of it!

I push the buggy to Manly Wharf to meet Kai at the earliest possible moment. When he wheels his bike off the Manly Fast Ferry ramp, he finds a broken woman. I cry for the rest of the evening. Even a Skype call with Mum and Dad doesn't make a dent in the awfulness of my feelings.

'How am I going to cope with a baby who cries all the time?' I sob to Kai.

'It was just one day, Jen. And you'll cope fine. You're a great mother.'

'I don't feel like one; everything seems just so *awful*!'

'It was probably just The Boy not being looked after properly by the staff at the crèche.

'Oh, God, what am I going to do?'

'You'll be fine, babes. I know you will.'

I go to bed exhausted from the heart-wrenching, stomach-churning misery.

Kai is working from home the following day. It's an awful day with me feeling desperately sad and anxious. And that was just the start of months of grinding misery.

Just after we left hospital I was assigned to a registrar (a trainee psychiatrist, Dr Paul McAllister) and I have weekly visits with the lovely Claudette. Dr Paul has curly hair around the sides of his head and a thin fringe of dead-straight hair brushed forwards over his receding hairline. In our first meeting, they told me I would definitely get better. They said all women with postpartum psychosis and postnatal depression do eventually get better, usually by the time their baby is six months old. 'Time', they told me. 'You just need to give it time.' We arrange to see each other again in three weeks. I was just so glad to be out of the hospital I didn't think about it much. I thought the worst was over. I didn't see how things could get worse. But they did.

We ask for an emergency appointment after the depression strikes because I know that something is very badly wrong. Dr Paul says it is very common to have a period of depression after mania and delusions; the up must be followed by a down. Yin and yang.

However, despite the severity of my depression, he is very reluctant to put me on antidepressants due to the risk of a mood elevator pushing me back into mania. I'm only on 50mg of amitriptyline for weeks. This is a very low dose – the dose I was taking to get rid of my tension headaches, in fact. I find out later that this is too low a dose to work as an antidepressant.

A few weeks after being poleaxed by postnatal depression, Kai and I start seeing Dr Walker, the psychologist who had helped me recover from the headaches. I don't remember much about the first meeting, but I do recall his anger growing as I slump on my chair, dull and leaden, barely responding to his questions.

Kai tells me later that Dr Walker said that I was overmedicated and he was going to have a word with Dr Paul who, by pure luck, worked in the same unit. In my next meeting with Dr Paul, he suggests that we reduce the sedating antipsychotic medication and I came back more into the world.

I'm incredibly grateful that Dr Walker knew me before babies and illness, and could see the extreme change in my behaviour that was, in some part at least, down to the side-effects of the medication.

I still struggle to find the words to describe how awful the period of depression was. If I could, I would instruct the words to fly off the page and lodge themselves in your heart, your gut, and in your throat: lacerating, grinding, slicing, crushing, and stabbing. The words would scoop out your stomach and nestle inside you, leaving you hollow, numb, and scared. I won't leave them there for long; that would be cruel. I will leave them for just long enough for you to understand how bad depression feels, and how much pain I am in.

It gets so bad that my amazing mum flies out from the UK to help look after me. I am so glad she's coming, but deep down, fear that it's reinforcing my fear that I am mad, that it's reinforcing my old "Cry-Baby Onion" trope. That I am weak. That I can't cope. That I am vulnerable. But the reality is that I am so depressed I can't be left on my own. I am too frightened. My dad can't fly out with Mum; problems with his heart mean the long flight is not safe. Also, six weeks is too long a time for both Mum *and* Dad to be away from Jo.

I can remember feeling extremely relieved that she was coming, and the slight elevation in my mood as I hoped against hope that I would feel better when she got to Australia, that it would really help. But, though her arrival made a huge difference to us because I wasn't alone and terrified, her presence didn't lift my depression. And that isn't too surprising.

There is a lot of debate at the moment over the medical or biological model for depression as opposed to the psychosocial model. Some are pushing back against the medical explanation that depression is due to a chemical imbalance in the brain, and that drugs can readjust this. They are calling for a more holistic view of depression being a result of much more than brain chemistry gone awry, that it is – at least partly – the product of a person's lived experiences, our place in society, and the lack of connection in the world.

In many ways, Drs Walker and Paul represent this battle between the medical model of mental illness and the psychosocial model. Medication is the top priority in the medical model and other factors (like not being so heavily medicated that you can hardly string a sentence together) being more important on the other. I think the answer is finding a balance between the two models with medication being a very important tool in the "Recovery Toolbox" for many with mental health problems.

I think, like most complicated illnesses and conditions, the causes are multiple and interlinked.

But personally, my experience of depression was a very biological one. Feeling safer and less terrified because my mum was with me every day would have had an obvious beneficial effect, but it didn't change the biochemical processes happening in my brain.

So, the burst of warmth and happiness I felt at seeing her standing on our doorstep with her wide grin, was soon swamped by the overwhelming feeling of misery and hopelessness.

I forced myself to go to an exercise class at my local gym every Tuesday, as I knew there was such good evidence that exercise can help improve mental health. But I hated it, and normally I love exercise. I hated the teacher, I hated the music, I hated how hard it was, I hated my fellow exercisers who I assumed weren't suffering like I was. I even hated the texture of the floor in the corridor outside the studio, a sort of rough grey short-hair carpet.

But there was one thing that kept me going. The physical pain of exerting myself, in my lungs and muscles, was a distraction. It was a tiny distraction, but it did give me some relief for a precious minute or two.

I also forced myself to go to a mother and baby yoga class with two of my friends from mothers' group once a week. I didn't hate this class so much, but it was so, so hard to make myself go and then to survive being there. Just getting there seemed so difficult, so full of impossible decisions: should I drive or walk ... On the one hand, there was the huge, almost impossible task of getting the giant pushchair collapsed into the boot of the car, as well as the potential terror of not being able to find parking. On the other hand, an incredibly steep, utterly exhausting 25-minute walk home.

If you have never experienced anything more than the usual level of anxiety over relatively everyday things, it is probably hard to understand how difficult it was to contemplate these two options. In the run up to them, one or other of these tasks would loom as large as a mountain in my mind, a mountain that was shaking and cracking and about to discharge huge boulders of fear on top of me if I didn't make the right choice.

And once I'd decided to actually do one of them, forcing myself to do it, was more difficult than self-administering root canal surgery, sans anaesthetic.

And let's not forget mothers' group ... The Mariana Trench low-point of my week, would loom large every Tuesday morning at ten o'clock. Again, I would force myself to go, filled with anxiety beforehand. One day, one of the other mums had organised a baby first aider to come and talk to us. It was excruciating listening to all the things that can and do go wrong with new babies and toddlers, the chokings on cherry tomatoes, burns from unattended BBQs, drownings in paddling pools ... Even though all these dire warnings were all followed with instructions of what do in cases of emergency, it still caused my anxiety to peak, over and over again. I sat there sweating, my mum sat next to me, occasionally squeezing my hand. She whisked me off afterwards to go for a decompressing walk along the ocean front.

In a strange way, the bad bits weren't so much worse ... it was all so bad. *Everything* was bad. When your mood is scoring minus a million, having an hour or two at minus a million and a bit hardly makes that much difference.

Days blend into weeks. Kai manages to go into work, despite being heartsick with worry for me. Mum helps me struggle through each hour, trying to comfort me when the waves of sadness crash through me. I beg to be allowed back into hospital, convinced that it's the only way I'm going to be able to cope.

The incredible, soul-aching misery turns even simple tasks, like getting out of bed or making dinner, into feats to be attempted only with great courage and support. It feels overwhelmingly pointless to shower when you'll only have to have another one the next day. Choosing clothes to wear is almost impossible, meaning that I wear the same collection of things week in, week out – a shabby capsule wardrobe for the depressed.

It's hard work looking after a small baby at the best of times, but when you're wracked with depression, things can seem hopeless. I try my best to play with my son, sing him songs, and smile at him as I see the other mothers around me doing with their babies, the way that Kai or Mum do with him, but my smiles are hollow and empty. It is very hard to sing 'If you're happy and you know it, clap your hands' when you are dying inside. I once started singing it to The Boy only to dissolve into tears. I still can't listen to that song without it giving me a chill.

It gets so bad that I finally understand how people are driven to end their own lives. I'd always thought that people who attempted (or succeeded in) suicide were doing it to hurt others, that it's an act of violence and anger towards the people left behind. But now I've experienced the searing emotional pain of severe depression for myself, I have a different view: that, for some people, the pain is just too much.

The urge to stay alive is incredibly strong in human beings, hardwired into our brains by hundreds of thousands of years of evolution. Generation after generation, our ancestors who had the stronger will to live were more likely to survive and pass their genes to their descendants. People will survive under extraordinary circumstances: extreme pain, extreme isolation, situations that don't just seem hopeless, but actually (by all reasonable analysis) *are* hopeless.

But people don't give up. They go on, endure, and survive. Whether it is a mountaineer dragging his broken body down a glacier (like Joe Simpson, whose true story is told in *Touching the Void*) or the many women, like Tamara Breeden or Elisabeth Fritzl, who were held prisoner and repeatedly raped and beaten for years before their escapes (some bearing children and raising them in windowless rooms), or the incredible drive to survive of those facing the devastation of war, the strength of the human spirit in these circumstances is astonishing.

But depression can eradicate this seemingly indestructible human urge so that, not only does a person not want to live, they will take action to ensure they don't.

Suicidal thoughts are more common than most people think (32% of adults who felt stress at some point in their lives had experienced suicidal thoughts, according to one report.[1]) and are a very common symptom of depression. The fact is that most people who attempt suicide don't want to die. They just want the pain to stop.

All the people around me are saying, 'This will end, hold on and give it time.' I don't believe them. The feeling of misery feels so permanent, so forever. Even with this assurance (which not

1. Mental Health Foundation (May 2018). Stress: Are we coping?
London: Mental Health Foundation

all people with depression have), the pain is so bad on my really bad days that I do consider the way out that suicide presents. The thought frightens me so much. But, luckily, it is a fleeting one, immediately squashed by the horror of the hurt and pain it would cause the people in my life, especially Kai, my parents, my sisters and, most of all, my son.

CHAPTER 25

FALLING ON MY HEAD
LIKE A MEMORY

Jo has made many suicide attempts, but the most serious one occurred 15 or so years ago. I was working in Sainsbury's at the time, as a marketing assistant on a temporary contract while I saved money for a trip to California and Mexico. It was just past two o'clock in the afternoon, and I was standing at the printer when I heard my phone go off in my bag. It was Mum.

'Jo's taken a turn for the worse.'

'What happened?'

'Another suicide attempt, I'm afraid.'

I gripped the phone tightly. The pit of grief opened up in my stomach, taking me back through the years, through the sadness and the pain.

'Where is she?'

'In a hospital in Oxford. A&E.'

I had just told my parents that I wanted to help support them more with Jo, so we agreed to tag-team it, with me going down that day, and them coming the following day. I took the rest of the day off and rushed to Paddington to get the next train to Oxford.

When I arrived at the hospital, Jo's friends, Tom and Tracey, were on either side of her bed in a curtained cubicle. Jo was sitting, propped up by two unyielding hospital pillows. Tom looked at me then back at Jo.

'Look, your sister's here.'

Jo's eyes were enormous, and her hands flickered and twitched with straight fingers. The rest of her, however, was still and frozen. There were globs of blood on the wall. She was wearing my bottle-green VB T-shirt (a treasured memento from my backpacking trip to Australia after university). I had been mystified by its disappearance a year or so ago. This triggered something in my brain. All the pain exploded inside me, and I was suddenly furious with her for it. My hands clenched into fists.

How could she? After all these years she is still managing to borrow my clothes without asking!

Back before she was ill, when we were both teenagers, she once borrowed a favourite top of mine and ruined it with melted plastic from a bag of bread that had got too close to the toaster. She'd just put it back in my wardrobe, melted plastic and all. Mum, Jo, and I had an almighty row about it, with Mum and me saying she couldn't borrow any more clothes, and Jo in tears. We'd always been a peaceful family, and sorted out disagreements without shouting. That is, we were until Jo hit adolescence. Her strong will was the rock to the hard place of my mum's parental control.

'It was an accident! I didn't do it on purpose.'

'That's not the point,' countered Mum.

'You always leave me out! You don't love me as much as I love you. And you definitely don't love me like you love Jen.'

She was never jealous of Tania; the age gap between us meant that sibling rivalry only existed between the two of us.

Tom took me out into the corridor, where we were surrounded by pained groans and the brisk nurses and doctors whisking past and disappearing into various cubicles. The smell of hospital – part antiseptic, part fear – crept into my nostrils and smoked up to my brain.

Tom was looking at me.

'Did you hear me?'

'Sorry, what?'

'Don't you want to know what happened?'

'Yes, sorry. I'm listening.'

He sighed. 'She said it was just all too much. You know she'd been working in the pub? Well, they found out and it looks like she is going to have to pay back a ton of money and lose her unemployment benefits.'

My chest contracted as I thought about the life my sister was living. Having so little money for so long that she'd justified cheating the system.

Tom was silent for a moment, watching my face.

'She called me. She was in a terrible state and when I got around to her flat, I found her passed out, and all these empty medication packs and a half-drunk bottle of vodka.'

My anger drained away and was replaced with a mix of pity and compassion. *The desperation she must have experienced, the pain* ... I opened the curtain and went to her side. I held one of her flickering, twitching hands.

'It'll be alright,' I told her.

She gabbled some nonsensical words at me, looking intently into my eyes. Her hands were raised, and she held her fingers rigidly at an angle, rippling her fingers as she talked.

'What has the doctor said?' I asked Tracey.

'None of them will talk to us.' She shrugged.

Pulling open the curtain again, I stepped out and looked around for a doctor or someone to ask.

'Excuse me,' I tried with one likely looking woman, but she ignored me. I tried again with a passing nurse, but with no success. After the third failed attempt to stop someone, I began to get angry. I grabbed the next doctor to go past by his elbow, gripping it tightly. He had short brown hair, thin metal-framed glasses and a square clenched jaw.

'Please, help me. I need to find out what is happening with my sister.'

His eyes darted to my sister's cubicle behind me.

'The overdose?'

'*My sister!*'

The labelling around medical conditions is extreme, especially for mental health issues. I guess it's a way for the doctors to compartmentalise the daily circus of physical and mental pain they witness. If they cared about each person as fully as a loved one does, they wouldn't be able to do their jobs, especially under the pressure which most Accident and Emergency departments operate. But calling a patient "the overdose" to that person's loved one … that moves away from self-preservation into callous indifference. It made my blood boil with rage at the time, and it still does now.

'I've got other patients. I'll be with you as soon as I can.' And he brushed past me.

My eyes filled with angry tears and I dialled Mum's number on the mobile. *If anyone could get the doctor to take me seriously, it would be Mum.*

'They won't tell me what's going on. She is in a terrible state,' I told her tearfully.

'Let me see what I can do,' said Mum before ringing off.

Ten minutes later, the same doctor came to find me. I noticed his bloodshot eyes and the pale grey skin around his mouth. His breath smelt of coffee and cigarettes.

'I've just spoken to your mother,' he informed me. 'Sorry I brushed you off earlier; I thought you were just another one of her druggy friends.'

'What do you mean?'

'Well she has clearly taken some recreational drugs as well as all the medical drugs. Probably ecstasy.'

'My sister doesn't do drugs!' She'd promised me never again after the last time she was in hospital. I trusted her. The only solution to this was that the doctor must have made a mistake. He was rushed. He was tired. He'd made a mistake.

There was a silence.

'She needs to be admitted to the psychiatric ward,' he explained. 'We're just waiting for the duty psychiatrist.'

'Is she going to be okay? Physically, I mean?'

'Yes, we think so. Her friend found her pretty soon after she'd taken the overdose, from what he said.'

'Thank you for talking to me.'

He rubbed his nose where his glasses rested and closed his eyes for a moment. Then, giving me a quick smile, he walked away down the corridor.

I went back into the cubicle, and a look of pure fear flashed across Jo's face when she saw me. I took her hand again anyway.

'Well?' asked Tracey.

'The doctors say you are going to be okay,' I said to Jo. 'We are just waiting for the duty psychiatrist.'

Then, I turned to Tom. 'It's lucky you got there so quickly! How did you get in if she was passed out – did you have to bust down the door?'

Tom looked away from me. 'Keys. I've got keys.'

He must have meant more to my sister than he was letting on.

It gave me a small flowering of happiness for my sister that, in among this pain, she had someone in her life.

There was a silence as we all looked at Jo. She tried a small smile and burbled something about birds and freedom.

'The doctor also said she was on something.'

Neither of them said anything.

'I'm getting a coffee,' said Tracey. 'Do you want one?'

I stayed for another three hours until the psychiatrist came and started the process of getting Jo admitted to the psych ward – the start of another of her long stays in hospital. I never found out if she had taken drugs, but being jerked into my sister's troubled and stressful life for a few hours was enough to make me heartbreakingly sad for weeks afterwards.

My brush with madness has given me insight into how tough things are for my sister. What I experienced for a few weeks, she has had to live with for months on end. My one week in hospital compared to years of being locked up for her.

This brings up many complicated feelings for me. On the one hand, I have much deeper insight into what it is like to experience psychosis, particularly delusions that feel completely and fundamentally real.

For example, when I thought that the book *Lucky Jim* was based on my dad, I believed this "fact" to be 100% true. When he said that it wasn't actually based on him, it caused me to frantically search for some other explanation. I believed it to be true, but my dad said it wasn't (and I knew he wasn't a liar) so there had to be some third explanation. At the time, I described this to myself as "the third way" – and three is the magic number, remember? The number three took on great significance for me, partly due to (or perhaps because of) this. As someone who loves science and rationality, I am comfortable with the notion that there are many things that I personally (and indeed humans as a whole) don't understand. The job of a scientist is to create hypotheses and collect evidence to test them out, trying to keep an open mind about the possible outcomes.

I think this scientific, rational approach to my thinking is part of what saved me from descending into paranoia about my family when they kept disproving the "facts" I knew to be true. An understanding that I can't know everything (and a lack of fear of this not knowing) is deeply embedded into my way of thinking. This understanding is also reinforced with the strong belief that I am clever, and I can work things out myself, thanks to my "flies make peanut butter" upbringing, along with incredible bonds of love and trust with my mum, dad, Jo, Tania and Kai.

So, you might think that this would give me acres of capacity to deal with my sister when she is saying deluded or untrue things. Unfortunately, it doesn't.

Recently, my sister told my family, including my son who is now six, that her flatmate had a gun and was planning to shoot my parents. I do understand how strongly she believed it when she said it. But she had no concept that it wasn't an appropriate thing to say in front of a small child – she was so immersed in her delusion that all thought of others flew from her mind. It is incredibly painful to remember how that felt, knowing that I have done the same thing to my family.

My immediate reaction was a complex mixture of emotions, as is often the way when something bad happens with my sister. First, there is anger at her for saying something like that in front of my son, then relief when it is obvious The Boy hasn't noticed at all, then wishing my sister wasn't ill, then guilt that I'm angry at her when she can't help it, and deep sadness that her reality is so filled with fear and pain. All whooshed up together in a delightful emotion cocktail and served over ice.

Even if The Boy hadn't been there I would have been stumped to know how to respond to it. Later that day, out of the blue she piped up, 'Remember that time you got a grant from the Prince's Trust?'

I had a choice: to go along with what she said, and not make a big deal of it, or contradict her.

Almost without thinking, I said, 'I never received a grant from the Prince's Trust, Jo.'

I contradicted her because I just couldn't help myself. She turned away from me, stony faced.

We were in a café at the time. It was one of Jo's favourite cafés in Oxford, but I find the multitude of clocks they have decorated the café with unsettling, like a surreal, Alice-in-Wonderland-esque alternate reality. Later, after we'd had lunch, Kai had taken The Boy outside to run around a bit, leaving Jo and I sitting on the same side of our booth. I was against the wall with no way of escape. My sister stirred her tea and stared into the middle distance, settling into the vinyl covered seat. Ignoring my question about what we should do next, she let loose a string of rambling, incoherent wrongs that people had done (and were doing) to her. As she continued her rant, it became clear that I was one of those people. I'm pretty sure my disagreement with one of her "facts" contributed to me being included in the group of people that made her feel paranoid in that moment.

I let her vent because I remembered how valuable my conversations with Lautaro were for "getting the crazy out". But it was hard to see her like that, and incredibly unsettling to know I had been like that too ... and that I could even become like that again.

Life is complicated, no?

*

On my way back to London after leaving her in the psychiatric ward, I realised how shit her life is most of the time, and it filled me with grief. I grieved for what could have been if she'd not become ill. Or if what they'd said when she had her first breakdown had been true – that she would get better in a matter of weeks.

The sound of the wheels on the tracks hummed in the background as the train sped along. I rang Mum, crying quietly.

'It was so awful.'

'We should have gone down ourselves; I didn't realise how bad it was going to be.'

'I need to be able to help with these things, though.'

'No, Jen, it was a mistake on our part.'

They go down the next day and set about getting her flat cleared up and her cats looked after by a friend. A sad routine with which they are painfully familiar.

I never see Tom or the T-shirt again.

CHAPTER 26

I'M GONNA KNOCK YOU OUT. MAMA SAID KNOCK YOU OUT.

A typical day. I wake up with the now-familiar feeling of dread pinning me to the pillow. I'm completely wiped out from the heavy medication, but I don't feel able to carry on sleeping. My dose of olanzapine (the mood stabiliser and antipsychotic) has been reduced from 20mg to 10mg, which makes a big difference, but I am still incredibly drowsy every morning.

I can hear Kai giving my son his early-morning bottle and my mum coming in from next door. (She is staying in the spare room of our kindly next-door neighbours, as we don't have space in our apartment; our old spare room is now The Boy's.)

The soft murmur of voices filters through the wall as she and Kai chat. I lie there, willing myself to get up and start the day, but I feel so sad that I just want to pull the covers over my head and never, ever get up again.

Get up. Get up. GET UP! I shout silently to myself.

Eventually, I force myself out of bed, flapping the duvet over and swinging my feet to the floor.

Then I go and sit on the sofa, eating a bowl of Weetabix. Mum tries to chat with me about plans for the day. I try my very best to answer her questions rather than being consumed by the feeling of misery and dread. Some mornings I have plans, such as an exercise class at the gym, mum-and-baby yoga, or mothers' group. Mum looks after The Boy while I get ready. I prepare myself and the nappy bag, and I'm ready at least an hour before I need to go. I then sit waiting on the sofa for the time to tick away, with my son sitting on Mum's lap while I try to fight off the feelings of anxiety and waves of sadness.

One of the worst things about the depression is that I feel no joy when I look at my son. I love him fiercely, but it is a grim, determined, come-what-may type of love, not the joyful, brimming-with-happiness-love that I felt in the early days. (It'll be months before I feel that again.)

If I have no plans, Mum and I go for a walk and try to get my son to sleep in the buggy. I've sat on most of the benches in Manly, Fairlight, and Balgowlah Heights, from Forty Baskets to Shelley Beach, with my mum holding my hand while I fight back the tears.

We come back to the flat for a lunch of soup and fruit. I can barely sit straight and spoon the soup into my mouth. It slides down my throat and lands in my churned-up stomach, making me feel sick. After lunch, I allow myself an hour to lie in bed. Sometimes I sleep, but mostly I lie there willing the time to pass. Then another walk in the afternoon, weather permitting. The minutes drag.

I hear my watch ticking and look again at the time, barely believing that only 15 minutes has passed since I last looked. Each minute is like an hour, each hour like a day, and each day like a week. I wait and wait all day for the sun to go down so I can go to bed. That is all I have to look forward to.

I'd spent many years doing yoga and trying to meditate, with the intention of living in the now and of being fully present. Before my son was born, I'd found that if I was able to live in the now, even for a short time, it was relaxing and fulfilling. It felt like living life intensely and to the full.

But what if the present sucks? Really hard?

For Kai, the psychosis and mania were the hardest to deal with because of the vicious arguments and the unpredictability. But for me, the depression was by far the worst of my experiences. Even though the psychosis and mania were terrifying and confusing at times, they came and went, so I would have periods where I felt "normal". Not only that, but elements of the mania brought feelings of intense joy and happiness.

On the other hand, my depression was overwhelming, unrelenting pain from the moment I woke up until the last hour of the day, to the slight lift before the wonderful oblivion of dreamless, drugged sleep.

Well, maybe not the exact moment I woke up. There were a few seconds of wakefulness (say, the first breath) before the pain swept in. But by the time that first lungful of air had been released, I was back in the unbelievable hell that my waking life had descended into.

In 'Lost My Mind' by Elley Duhe, she sings,

Please always love me

Even though I lo-, I lo-, I lost my mind

Then there is a beat followed by:

Wake up, survive

This is really what it felt like, a beat of calm then extreme pain and the start of what truly felt like a fight to survive every minute of every hour.

This went on for endless day after endless day.

*

I don't know how to struggle through anymore.

It is so, so painful. Throughout the day, my sadness peaks and overflows. I sob and cry, begging someone to do something to help me. My mum holds and comforts me, trying to get me to feel at least a bit better. We are both exhausted by the time Kai is back from work. After dinner, I have a few hours where my mood lifts slightly and I watch an hour or so of TV before collapsing into bed, already dreading the following morning.

And the next day, the same things would happen.

And the same, the day after.

And the same, the day after.

I have to fight and fight every day just to do normal things. The effort exhausts me, and that, combined with the medication, means I long for bedtime and the self-extinguishing relief of sleep.

On and on it goes, till the days link up and make weeks. And the weeks and weeks turn to months.

At the end of Mum's six weeks, we plan to fly back to England for a three-month "baby tour".

I'm still vulnerable, insecure, and depressed, but things are at least a little better than when she first arrived. Time and effort mixed with kindness and love have started sanding off the sharp edges of the pain. I am just about able to consider a 24-hour flight back to London, something that would have been impossible in the early stages of the depression.

Through grim determination, I learn that staying at home doesn't make things any easier. Being out and about, either because of the change of scenery or the company, sometimes helps distract me and gives me respite from the gloom for a short while.

I remember the first break I had in the depression. It lasts 15 minutes. I am out walking with my son, and there are banks of large, structural clouds filling up the blue, blue sky.

Swallows swoop and wheel overhead. I close my eyes and feel the warmth of the sun on my face, and something seems to melt inside me. The grip that misery has around my heart loosens.

I stop walking. I feel (and I can hardly believe it) ... I feel okay! It is such a contrast to how I've been feeling for weeks that the sensation is totally amazing. I don't know what to do.

This is how life used to be. I freeze on the spot, unwilling to move in case the feeling goes away. I look around me, willing the feeling to stay.

Hope blooms in my chest. *Maybe it is ending. Maybe, maybe ...*

But then, like a cog turning, time moves on and the warm glow fades. The familiar, grey, suffocating feeling returns, and it feels worse than before now I've had a taste of how things used to be. I turn the buggy around and run back home with tears rolling down my cheeks.

Later that week, I talk to Claudette about it. She says that, though it is hard to have such a good feeling come then go, this is what my recovery is probably going to feel like. She tells me I'll have more and more times feeling okay and then they'll start to last for longer and longer. I, of course, don't believe her. She says that it would be worrying to get better really fast as the risk would be of tipping over into mania. Slow and steady is best.

When we arrive in London, I book in to see my wonderful GP, the same one I have had since I was a child. She refers me immediately to a specialist perinatal mental health unit in Homerton Hospital. Thanks to the vagaries of both the NHS admin systems and the UK postal system, my referral letter gets lost, so I don't get an appointment until halfway through my stay in the UK. But when I do get to see a psychiatrist, she immediately increases the dose of the antidepressant I'm on. She says the amount I was taking won't have made a difference to my depression, as it is below the therapeutic dose.

This doesn't mean very much to me at the time; in many ways, I just take the news as another piece of "bad luck", like the fact that my referral letter got lost. But in retrospect, it makes me furious that the psychiatrist in Australia had left me to battle severe depression without effective medication. While I know some people don't like to take antidepressants (many are concerned, quite rightly, with an over reliance of antidepressants in the medical profession, with some (Scott Lilienfield et al.) arguing that the term itself is greatly misleading), I do respond to them, and the fact that I wasn't given the chance to try them when I needed them most only caused me and my family more suffering.

The UK psychiatrist also quickly weans me off one of the mood stabilisers. Apparently, the risk of birth defects mentioned by my St Anne's consultant, Toby, is in fact so severe that UK doctors don't give it to women, even if they're not planning to get pregnant (accidents can happen!). She also refers me to a psychologist who tries to get me to see that I can cope, and have been coping. She is kind, patient, and understanding. We have many useful conversations over the few weeks during which I see her in her drab, beige office. I remember one conversation about what I used to enjoy doing.

'Yoga, reading, hanging out with friends, writing.'

'Writing?' she asks.

'Yep, I did an MA in Professional Writing.'

'Why don't you try writing now?'

'Well it won't make me feel any better.'

'Then you have nothing to lose.' She sits smiling at me and a smile inches up my own cheeks too.

'I can't argue with that,' I concede.

So, I start writing every day while The Boy takes his morning nap. Not only does it help, but this book is the result of that daily writing practice.

I make slow progress though the ebbs and flows of depression and, while I have some terrible, terrible times, day by day I can feel myself inching towards equilibrium. I carry on my campaign to get out and meet people every day, no matter how bad I feel. It is hard, hard work, but since I have no choice, I get my head down and get on with life. As Churchill said, 'When you are going through hell, keep going.' I start having hours in the day when the soul-wrenching misery lifts. These hours start becoming more and more common. Some of them link together and I start having whole mornings or afternoons when ... well, I wouldn't say I felt good, but I didn't feel bad.

When I do have my regular setbacks, it feels like I'm starting from scratch. Sometimes, I think that this is what it's going to be like forever, despite what anyone says to me. I have a great reluctance to believe the low period will end. I think this is so deeply ingrained in me because of what happened to my sister.

I see Jo and try to explain what has been happening to me. I am raw with nerves about seeing her. I feel so vulnerable, and I worry about how I'll deal with her if she isn't having a good day. But she is full of sympathy and understanding. She tells me that I am a good mum and a strong woman, and I will get through this. She wants to keep me company, and comes to stay in London. I struggle with this, like I am struggling with everything. I find it stressful to be around her when I am feeling low; I feel I'm letting her down in some way. But I think the deep reason is that, even when she is doing well, she needs a lot of emotional support and understanding, and I'm just not in a position to be able to give it to her.

I want to express to her how I have a much better understanding of her and her illness now, but the words come out jumbled or clichéd. I am too wrapped up in my own hopelessness to give her any support. I go and see her twice at her home in Didcot, where she lives. She plans to come down to London again, but pulls out at the last minute.

At one point, we worry that things are starting to go wrong for her and alert her support team. Mum and Dad are exuding the expectation of Impending Bad Times. Sometimes, I wonder about my choice to live so far away from my family. *Is there an element of escape to it?* I now realise there must be.

But there are some good times too, especially towards the end of my stay. Claudette was right: the breaks come more and more frequently and last longer and longer. I have a truly amazing support network in London, made up of my friends and those of my parents. It's like a safety net hanging underneath me as I walk the tightrope of recovery. I meet up with old friends, get swept along in the 2012 Olympics euphoria, and drink real ale in real pubs. One friend, who doesn't realise how bad I'm feeling, pulls me up for not including her early enough in an invitation to a local park, but other than that, all is good. I meet up with Tania and her family, and go to galleries and museums with Mum and Dad. I manage these things despite still being haunted by the ghost of depression, and try not to get disheartened when the good times turn to bad.

There is one friend, who I have known since we were both in playgroup, who is recovering from brain cancer and so not working. Despite everything she's going through, she arranges to see me once a week. One time, I'm so wracked with anxiety about travelling up to see her on the bus that her amazing dad (who I've also known since I was a toddler) offers to come and get me.

Another friend, an old colleague of mine, meets up with me a few times too. The strength of our connection and my determination to focus on the "well" version of me helps me start to find the light at the end of the tunnel. Light that I determinably trudge towards, hoping against hope that I will reach it soon.

Progress is slow and painful, but by the end of the three months I am 80% back to normal, and mostly able to cope on my own. The best thing is that I start to really enjoy being with my son rather than being frightened of looking after him.

CHAPTER 27

I'VE SEEN THIS ROOM AND I'VE WALKED THIS FLOOR

As our time in England draws to an end, I start looking forward to getting back to Australia and getting back to a routine. I start daydreaming about how I will spend the last few months of my maternity leave, now that I am starting to feel at least somewhat better. I imagine spending my time in ways that (I assume) other new mums do, without the terrible fear and pain piercing every moment. Maybe I will make brownies, while my son plays on his rug. Or I might take a stroll down the walkway from Manly Beach to the small golden curl that is Shelley Beach, where I'll put a rug down and chill with my baby. I am tired of living out of suitcases and other people's homes. I want my apartment back and my own stuff around me.

I feel we are ready to start moving on with the rest of our lives. But it turns out the rest of our lives isn't quite ready for us.

We'd been warned the jet lag could have a negative effect on my progress, so we shouldn't have been blind-sided by it, but in the first few weeks back in Australia, I take a dramatic turn for the worse.

The first day I have on my own, I take a walk down to Shelley Beach, the buggy loaded up with a rug, some toys for The Boy, and my book. The water is shining and shockingly blue, wavelets reflecting the light in spangles. The air is fresh and bright. People are milling around on the walkway, buzzing with energy. Across the water, I can see the surfers paddling to Fairy Bower.

We get to the beach and I lay out the rug, but somehow, I can't get comfortable on the sand. Everywhere I sit, there are twigs sticking through the blanket and digging into my thighs. There is no shade free and we are in the baking sun. I've smothered The Boy in sun cream, and within minutes, sand and small bits of leaves and twigs have invaded the rug. One or two rolls later, The Boy is coated with sand and detritus like an angry, gritty, baby goujon. He refuses to keep his hat on. Every time I put in on, he rips it off and throws it away. We battle over the hat for a few minutes before I give up. Around us, backpackers lounge and party. I'm so hot, but I don't want to take us both into the sea, as my handbag with wallet, phone, and keys would be easy pickings for a beach thief.

The dread rises in my throat. It is all shit. Nothing is like it was before. *Having a baby ruins everything.*

I quickly repack the bag and struggle to get a hot and ferocious The Boy back into the stroller. Have you ever tried to push a fully loaded pushchair over soft sand? Easy it is not. Ten minutes of pulling, pushing, and shoving gets me back to the walkway. Sweat drips down from my underarms and soaks into my bikini sides. Stopping for a moment in a patch of blessed shade, I look back at everyone else on the beach having fun, relaxing, laughing, splashing in the shallows. My daydreams lay shattered around my feet like crushed-up shells, sharp and painful.

The hopelessness and gloom descend again on the walk back, obliterating the sparkling sunshine of springtime in Sydney. I don't even try to bake brownies. I've never baked a sodding brownie in my life! Who was I kidding?

The next day, I call Claudette in tears to tell her how I'm feeling, and ask for a meeting with Dr Paul.

The next Friday morning, I grip Kai's hand as we sit waiting outside the office. I am rocking the buggy backwards and forwards, trying to get my son off for his morning sleep. I feel dreadful: numb, yet in pain at the same time.

Dr Paul calls us into his office, where Claudette is sitting waiting for us, and asks how I'm doing. This triggers the tears that have been gathering in the corners of my eyes.

'I just feel so *awful* again. I thought it was over!'

'Can you tell me what medication you're on?'

He is holding the long letter written by the psychiatrist in London.

'They took me off the mood stabilisers because it isn't recommended in the UK, and upped the antidepressant to 100mg.'

'Well, I think we need to get you back on the sodium valproate to start with.'

'No, I don't want to start taking it again.'

'Is it because you are thinking of getting pregnant? There is no harm in taking it unless you are.'

'No, we're not thinking of getting pregnant, but it just feels like such a step back. And I don't want to be even more tired than I am already.'

'It's about getting you better as fast as possible.'

'I think I just need a higher dose of antidepressant.'

'Yes,' agrees Kai. 'We think that will do the trick.'

'They told me that the 50mg I was on was too low a dose to work as an antidepressant. Why did you have me on such a low dose?'

'Let's not worry about that now.' He dismisses me, then floors me with his next words.

'Bipolar,' he says. 'I think you have a vulnerability to bipolar.'

I start to sob. *No, no, no. I can't have bipolar!* The only other person I knew with that had killed herself the year before. I am devastated. It can't be true. I am not suicidal right now, but if I'm bipolar, does it mean I might be again?

But, underneath my shock and desperate hurt, I always knew this would happen. The latent pessimist in me opens one bleary eye and sits up. *See*, it tells me, *you knew you'd get ill like Jo – and lo and behold, you were right!*

My pessimism about myself and what my life will be crystallises into this one point in time. All my fighting, all the reassurance that I wasn't going mad like my sister, all is dealt a death blow by this doctor who's spent no more than five hours in my presence over the months of my illness.

Claudette is squirming in her seat.

'It's okay, Jen,' murmurs Kai.

'No! No, it isn't.'

'Jennifer,' says Dr Paul.

'I can't believe it! This is so awful.'

'You've never mentioned about bipolar before,' says Claudette, frowning. 'She only had one episode of mania when she was having the psychosis.'

'Well, either it is bipolar or a major depression.'

'Why not postnatal depression?' I ask, still crying.

'If it continues on past six months, then it is no longer called postnatal depression.'

My heart sinks even further. I am in month seven.

By the end of the meeting, we haven't agreed on my medication plan. We insist that I don't want to start taking sodium valproate again, and that I do want to increase the antidepressant. Dr Paul finally agrees, but says I should double the antipsychotic and mood stabiliser. This would have put me back to 20mg, the amount I was on when Dr Walker had to intervene as I was overmedicated.

I say yes to the increase at the time, but thinking about it later that night, I decide not to up the dose. Dr Paul says he will get a second opinion from one of the more senior psychiatrists at the centre.

At the end of the session, he says, 'I do want to apologise about the way I handled this session, Jennifer. I had forgotten how sensitive you are because of your sister.'

I say nothing, merely staring at him. With one stroke, he has diagnosed me with a severe, lifelong mental health condition. He has so much power over me; I don't want to antagonise him further. My normal, assertive self was battered and beaten, but I still wonder, *So it's my fault for being sensitive, is it? I see*.

We file out of the room and set up a follow-up meeting. Claudette rests her hand on my shoulder and gives me a reassuring smile. 'Remember, it's just words. Just a label.'

But her words don't comfort me. It's interesting – negative comments and bad news stick, but it's much harder to hear and take reassuring words, especially when we are in a crisis.

The following day, Saturday, I have a session with Dr Walker, where I explain what happened with Dr Paul.

Dr Walker is sitting with his legs crossed and his hands gripping his upper knee.

'I don't think you have bipolar,' he says.

His words make me feel weak with relief. Suddenly, light blooms at the end of the tunnel of darkness into which Dr Paul's diagnosis had plunged me. *Maybe everything is going to be alright after all*.

'You can see why people and situations get medicalised, but there are lots of reasons why you are feeling particularly sad at the moment. I think what's happening to you now is situational rather than biological.'

I am silent, listening intently. It feels vitally important that I absorb every word he says.

'When you were first ill, that was definitely caused by brain chemistry, but now I think you are experiencing normal emotions – you're just not processing them. You have a bad or uncomfortable feeling and you think the worst. It makes you panic.'

'I do. I totally fucking panic.'

'Your challenge is recognising – and accepting as normal – down or anxious feelings that we all have, and not worrying that you are getting ill again.'

In my recovery, this has been one of the hardest things to try to do. For example, imagine that a friend says or does something that I think is thoughtless and hurtful. But because I'm not sure, I doubt my own reaction to it. I question whether maybe I'm having this emotion, not because of what they said or did, but because I'm getting ill again. It's like I'm gaslighting myself. And it's made worse when other people, who know about my mental health experience, ask the same thing – 'Do you think it's because your medication's not working?' I'm thinking it, they're thinking it ... sometimes it feels like I'm being gaslit by everyone around me, including myself. "Masslit", if you will.

'You're experiencing a lot of loss at the moment. You've lost the close support of your family and friends in London. You've had months of direct support from your mum, and from your dad when in London, too, and now you're mostly on your own again. Anyone would be feeling a bit lost.'

It is such a relief to have someone countering Dr Paul's rigid, medical model approach, and it does make sense on an intellectual level. But you don't just erase years of thinking about yourself in a single session with a psychologist, however wise and brilliant they might be.

'That does make sense. Thank you. But how do I go about processing rather than panicking?'

'You can start by trying to look at the context when you feel sad. Just take a moment, and rather than panicking, think, 'What is going on that might make me sad or anxious?' Give yourself time to go through options. Then, once you've come up with one or two possible reasons, you can just accept the feelings for what they are. Hopefully this will stop you panicking and help you feel more in control of your emotions. We can work through some of the times when you've felt down, and I can help you see the context. It might be hard at first – in fact, I'm sure it will be – but the more you practise, the better you'll get at processing.'

'Okay.'

'So, can you think of a time you felt sad, down, or anxious?'

'Quite often, I get envious of the childless couples I see when I'm walking my son around Manly – they're just sitting on the beach, reading books, or just strolling around without a care. I feel so guilty that I'm jealous, almost like I'm wishing my son didn't exist, which makes me feel like the worst mother in the world.'

'Right, so we can see that one of your vulnerabilities is a feeling of envy. You must remember it is envy of a situation that you assume to be true, rather than one you know to be true.'

'What do you mean?'

'You assume the couples you see are happy, but they might not be. The couple reading might have run out of things to say to each other. They might be bored with each other, or ignoring each other after an argument.'

Understanding dawns on me.

'Oh, I see,' I say, and I really do. Something has just clicked.

I picture one couple I passed on one of my endless walks back and forth along the scenic walkway, pushing the stroller in front of me like a bow wave. *They are tanned, blonde, and perfect in that way that only Sydneysiders can be. Holding hands loosely. Laughing as I pass.* At the time I felt a stab of jealousy and misery, but in my mind's eye, as I remember them, I have the ability to look deeper and understand them more. I think about them as whole, unique individuals, with hopes, dreams, and difficulties just like me. Despite their beautiful exteriors, they are bound to face difficulties in life. Every single person does. Life is hard and confusing at times. As a wise person once told me, 'Don't judge your insides by someone else's outsides.'

'Yes, and the couple strolling might be desperate for children and might, in fact, be looking at you with envy.'

In my mind's eye again, I can see the couple as they continue walking down the path. The woman looks at the man and he looks down. A world of pain opens between them, of failed pregnancy tests, failed IVF, miscarriages, and once high hopes, breaking again and again as each month, a period arrives. Pain that I have no experience of. Pain that I can only imagine.

'Yes, that's true, they might.'

'This isn't to say you should comfort yourself meditating on the difficulties of others, but just acknowledge you don't know anything about what other people are going through. Okay. Any more?'

'Last week, I had a really bad day on Thursday. We had the car in the garage to get the air con fixed. They were supposed to finish on Wednesday but there was a delay and I had to pick it up later on Thursday. That meant I missed two events I had planned: a pool party at one of my friend's from mothers' group in the morning, and then lunch with my boss to talk about coming back to work. It seems like such a little thing, but it threw me into a whirl of misery, and feeling that my life is just so shit.'

'Okay, so this example makes me think you have a vulnerability to being disappointed, being let down and possibly letting down others in return.'

'Yes, I see that.'

'So, do you see how you can work through the situation and try to see the context?'

'Yes, I'll give it a try next time I feel sad.'

'Another thing which will help you is trying to anticipate situations which might make you feel sad or anxious, and trying to prepare yourself for them.'

'So, I often get sad on a Saturday morning – I think it's because I've been looking forward to the weekend so much that it makes me feel really sad when it comes and I don't feel as I expect I should about it.'

'Yes, so you might prepare yourself for that on Friday evening. Think about how you might be feeling the following day.'

'Okay, I'll try.'

I leave the session feeling light. The huge worry of the possibility of having bipolar is lifted slightly, though it still hovers around me. I also feel like I have more ways to help myself the next time I get sad.

At the meeting with Dr Paul on Monday, Kai and I stand our ground, and in the end, he agrees to keep the medication at the same dose.

'I consulted with the other psychiatrist who says that, though she can't diagnose without actually meeting you, she agrees with my assessment.'

I sit and look at him. I imagine the discussion they might have had and wonder how one-sidedly he would have presented my situation to her.

'Well, that's as may be,' I say. 'But I really don't want to take any more drugs than the ones I'm on already. We think that this set-back is due to psychological reasons, and taking more drugs would only do more harm.'

'Well, that is your choice. I just want to get you better as quickly as possible.'

'I'm already taking one mood stabiliser. I don't want to take another one.'

'The Black Dog Institute recommends up to three or four mood stabilisers for treatment-resistant depression.'

A stab of fear slices my stomach. Treatment-resistant – is that what I have?

'Nevertheless, we are just going to stick with the increase in antidepressants.'

'Okay,' he says.

'And I have to tell you that I didn't increase the dose of olanzapine as you suggested.'

He sighs and scribbles something in my notes. He seems to have accepted that I'm not going to do what he says. I leave feeling more in control.

We've been back in Sydney for three months now, and I'm feeling much more myself again. I haven't had to increase my meds beyond the increase in the antidepressant. I try to take each day as it comes and hope that soon I'll be totally back to normal. The low days I have now are so much easier than the low days I used to have. In a way, it feels good to only feel a bit bad. I'm noticing that the low periods are shorter and I'm more able to take action to make myself feel better, like doing some yoga while my son is asleep, or arranging to meet a friend for coffee (or tea in my case).

I have continued to have regular appointments with Dr Walker. He has supported me in learning how to recognise and accept some of the negative feelings I have, and to anticipate times when I might feel low to avoid getting into a panic. I've also continued to see Claudette. Her calm reassurance boosts my confidence and I look forward to her visits. I don't think I would have got better without the support of these two!

CHAPTER 28

IT'S A NEW DAWN, IT'S A NEW DAY, IT'S A NEW LIFE FOR ME

*Life just seems so fun and filled with possibilities. It is amazing –
I never thought I'd feel like this again.*

Email to a friend.

They talk about having a period of "adjustment" when you have a baby. The word "adjustment" brings to mind slightly moving the rear-view mirror to get a clearer view, or a tiny turn of the shower taps to get exactly the right temperature of water. Not the huge and all-encompassing changes that you go through when you have a baby.

It is hard for me to know what the experience of motherhood would have been like without being ill, but from talking to my friends with kids, they all found the adjustment to be hard, despite loving their children more than anything. The dual feelings of difficulty (and even resentment) mixed with overwhelming love is called "ambivalence". Ambivalence is extremely common, but generally not talked about openly. Mothers and fathers tend to feel guilty about their mixed feelings. They hide them from the world at large, talking only of the good times. I myself had strong feelings of ambivalence, which made me feel incredibly guilty and added to my depression.

There is such a taboo around saying how hard, and sometimes awful, being a parent is. When Rachel Cusk wrote about this in her book about motherhood, *A Life's Work*, she received harsh criticism, not on her writing, but on her very ability to love and care for her child. In the book, Cusk gives a completely honest account of how hard she found being a new mother, despite loving her child. In the introduction to a later edition, she tells of how she was criticised harshly by many reviewers and readers "who accused me of being an unfit or unloving mother, the critics who still use my name as a byword for hatred of children, the readers who find honesty akin to blasphemy when the religion is that of motherhood."

My own experience is that most women will complain about specific aspects of parenting rather than the whole. They will talk about the lack of time for themselves, for example, but then, when I agree, look up in alarm and say, 'But I wouldn't have it any other way.' Women will ask how old my son is, and then say, 'Ah what a lovely age,' their beaming smile floundering on their face when I find the only answer I can give is silence. It makes me feel all the more alone in my experience. Maybe I am just a bad mother and, though I love my son with all my heart, maybe other people love their children just that bit more than I do? Or maybe my life before having kids was "better" than theirs. Maybe they didn't revel in freedom and independence like I did? Or maybe everyone's experience of parenting, like every other experience in life, is unique to them and it is pointless trying to compare my experience with other mums.

Now I'm years away from the first wave of frontline parenting – years nought to three – I am enjoying it so much more. Despite all the crap, when people say 'What a lovely age', I know exactly what they are talking about. For me, being a mum has got better and better with each passing year. Maybe my period of adjustment to the new reality of my life just took longer than most people's. Thanks to a combination of my personality, my life experiences, and a decimating illness, I'm only just getting it.

It is similar to the taboo around mental health, in a way – not so much in origin but in outcome. This means lots of people suffer in silence. If more parents were brave enough to say how tough it is, then it might not be such a shock when people do have children of their own. They might also be ready to support each other through the tough bits.

I'm lucky that I had lots of friends who were very honest about the less-than-rosy side of parenthood. I remember talking to one friend who said that, when she thinks back to her life before kids, she feels a deep, deep grief over what she gave up. She says she would still make the same choice again because she wouldn't want her children not to exist, to essentially be dead, but she still recognises the huge loss she has experienced.

As we sat in Clissold Park, our sons rolling around on the picnic blanket, another friend said that she thinks all women experience some level of mental illness after they have a baby, in that the horror of the situation is so hard to bear that it basically turns all new mums crazy to a greater or lesser extent.

It is quite hard to comprehend just how much having kids changes your life before you have them. The sharp joy you feel when your child smiles at you, or rests his head on your shoulder when he is tired, mixed with the unending, monotonous work of looking after a baby – as well as the loss of freedom, especially when they are young – can be confusing and overwhelming.

One of the signs that I was getting better was that, even if I was having a tough day with The Boy, one cute heart-melting smile from him was all I'd need to feel full of all-encompassing, bright and beaming love.

The rest of the time, just the absence of the chest-squeezing and gut-wrenching misery makes the days almost joyous. It is such a relief to simply feel normal. If you have ever been camping with only cold water, you'll know the wonderful feeling of having a hot shower after days or weeks of roughing it. It is the same hot shower you have every day before work, but it feels so amazing and different.

It was the same feeling for me; something as normal as meeting a friend for coffee, or pushing my son on a swing, would feel so delicious and wonderful simply because the feelings of dread and misery were no longer pulling away at me.

The thing that my illness revealed to me is how deep my fear of "going mad" was, and how much stronger it was in me than in other people with mental ill health issues in their families.

I just thought that the level of fear I had was the normal amount for someone in my position, but I was wrong. For reasons deeply buried in my past, this fear was huge for me. If there is a silver lining of having psychosis, it is that I now feel that I have experienced a version of madness, and have survived. I didn't have to be sectioned. Though I went to hospital, it was only for a week, not for the months I feared it might be. In a strange way, despite everything, I feel so much stronger and more resilient now.

Or do I?

I do sometimes feel super-resilient – if I can survive this, I can survive anything. Sometimes. Other times I feel that my confidence in myself is like a vase that has been smashed, and the fractures in my being so weakly fixed that the slightest upset will break me again. I have painstakingly glued myself together over weeks and weeks of patient restitution, but the result is a self on the brink of falling to pieces. Each piece of the whole is weakly holding on to its neighbours for dear life. I hope this fragility wears away. I hope that I become stronger than the sum of my parts. I now look forward to my future, rather than dreading the coming day.

Mental illness should be treated by the world at large just like any other illness – no shame, no fear, no guilt, just ill health, which can be treated by medication in tandem with professional support. It is vital that any support is a mixture of these two, and that people realise that, in most cases, there is no magic pill that will make it all go away.

Mental ill health is so common; it's almost a cliché to say so. The Australian Bureau of Statistics carried out a *National Survey of Mental Health and Wellbeing in 2007* that found an estimated one in five Australians had a mental disorder in the 12 months prior to the survey. The UK charity, Mind, conducted a study that found that in Britain, it's one in four.

So then, why is the taboo still so strong?

It is not our fault that the taboo exists. It is just something about the way our society has evolved, springing as it has out of an understandable fear of all illnesses from a Darwinian I-want-my-genes-to-pass-on-to-the-next-generation perspective. The taboo is part of our society and, though it is getting better, each person is jointly and equally responsible for the way our society behaves. It isn't some mythical beast running on some unknowable power on its own. It is us. We can change it if we put our minds to it.

One way to break the taboo is for people with mental ill health to speak up and be honest about what is happening (or has happened) to them – though I want to be very clear: in no way do I want people who have lived experience to feel like they have to speak up if this isn't right for them or their families.

In one way, it is very easy for me to speak up about mental illness. I have had decades of close, personal experience of seeing how the taboo negatively affects my sister, and a burning desire to do something about it. It brings me great happiness to know at last that I can do something real and practical that might in some indirect way make my sister's life better.

I work in the voluntary sector, where I hope and believe there are more people who have an open and understanding view of the benefits that having a truly diverse workforce brings. That isn't to say there aren't "knobends" in the voluntary sector – there are plenty of them. But the ethos of the sector is about positive social change for the better, and breaking taboos of all kinds is part of this. I'm not a teacher, lawyer, or doctor who might get the sack if she wrote a book about being psychotic. Sure, it might have a negative impact on my career. But I don't fucking care.

Also, I had a magic combination of psychosis with postnatal depression (PND) – novel and "exciting" meets (sadly) common. It's a double whammy of a book. Some people are just born lucky, I guess!

One of the reasons I've written this book is because I hope that, by publicly detailing what has happened to me it will increase understanding of both PPP and PND. Specifically, I want to show that you can think you are Cameron Diaz, and you can believe you can control all dogs with your mind, and they *still don't take your kid away*. I hope this will encourage more women to not fear this, and to speak up if they are struggling. The more that women feel they are able to do this, the less suffering will occur.

Did you know suicide is a leading cause of death for women with a baby between 0 and 12 months? Despite all the things we know, and all the support that is available, there are babies growing up without mums, partners without their best friends, husbands without their wives, and grandparents without their daughters. Ultimately, I hope fewer mums will get to the point of extreme desperation and decide to end the pain by killing themselves. Suicide is a preventable cause of death. This book is part of my effort to help prevent it. I'm probably putting too much responsibility in one book, but here's hoping anyway.

If you, or a loved one, ever finds yourself in my position, my advice is to remember you do have rights. Unless you've been sectioned under the Mental Health Act, you don't have to stay in hospital if it is really not working for you. You also have a say in what medication you take, and the dose. This is really tricky as the doctors are, most definitely, the experts on medication and it helps if you trust them and the combination of drugs they want you to take. In general, it is best to take their advice, but remember you are the expert on you, and your personal experience. If something doesn't feel right, then you should attempt to trust your instincts. This is hard to do when your instincts have just been telling you that you are going to meet Barack Obama and catch all paedophiles. But it is still possible.

Part of getting better is learning to trust your instincts again, and this is what medical staff should focus on more.

I guess what I mean is that, whatever flavour your crazy is, remember you know you the best. Your partner, or parents, or whoever is your support network, are vital to working out the balance between listening to the doctors and listening to what your gut is telling you.

My other piece of advice is, try, if you can, to get yourself a Kai. I couldn't have survived the ordeal if I didn't have mine.

CHAPTER 29

MAKE A SPACE, FOR MY BODY, DIG A HOLE, PUSH THE SIDES APART

The depression takes months to even get to the stage where I can just about cope on my own. Every day is a battle, progressing slowly – very slowly. Some days I go back to feeling just as bad as I ever did, and have to gather my courage and start the process of getting better all over again.

How did I do it? Well, I'm still doing it.

Even as I write this, I'm not 100% better. I try to take each day as it comes – good, bad, or somewhere in between. I find it's easier to cope if I try not to worry too much about days in the future. It doesn't always work, but I try.

I feel we all need to protect our mental health as we do our physical health. Luckily, the things you need to do for one also work for the other. Here is what works for me:

1. **I have two mantras.** I repeat them over and over in my head, especially when I'm walking with my son in the buggy. Since I have been ill, sometimes a certain phrase of a song I've just heard will get stuck on a loop in my brain, repeating over and over and driving me to distraction.

When this happens, I find that repeating one or other of my mantras disrupts the annoying lyrics.

My mantras are:

'I am fit and strong and healthy.'

'I can cope with anything in this moment.'

I find the second one to be particularly helpful when I'm feeling really bad. The marvellous Claudette talked to me about "radical acceptance" and I have found that repeating the second mantra is a way to experience this. You try to just calmly and gently accept what is happening to you. Then, because you are not fighting it or struggling with self-pity, it actually makes things feel a bit better. It is quite hard to do, but once you get the hang of it, it works really well. It is all part of something I've been working on for years with yoga and meditation: being present and in the moment.

2. I exercise. I find this really helps my mood, particularly yoga, swimming, and walking. It is hard to find the time to exercise when you have a young baby, but life is much easier to cope with if you can keep active. The endorphins that are released after exercise work as a natural antidepressant.

At the moment, I do yoga on a Saturday morning so Kai can look after The Boy. We do an exercise DVD together most Monday evenings after my son has fallen asleep and before we start making dinner. On Thursdays, I do sessions with two mums from my mothers' group and a personal trainer. The trainer even helps to occupy the babies in their prams while we run around, do squats, sit-ups, and other exercises.

If the weather is nice, and I can fit it in, I also go swimming once a week.

Most days, I walk for at least an hour with my son in his buggy; it's good exercise, he gets lots of fresh air and it helps pass the time. Because he is such an active little soul, this is the only time out of the house that I can totally relax. Visiting other mums or having a picnic on a rug can be quite stressful with my son racing around putting bark, leaves, and whatever else he can find into his mouth, or trying to destroy a friend's living room.

3. **I have close times with Kai.** This can be a big hug, having a dance around the kitchen, or snuggling on the sofa, as well as sex. It really boosts my mood.

4. **I eat well and drink in moderation.** I make sure I eat a healthy balanced diet most of the time. I don't drink much alcohol; it doesn't agree with me as much as it used to. That being said, a lovely glass of wine or refreshing gin and tonic on a Friday evening is okay for me.

5. **I write.** I find that writing every day, if I can, helps. I usually manage to get an hour done when my son is asleep, though he has started becoming hard to settle. I try to settle him in his cot, but if this doesn't work, I sling him in the pushchair, or baby seat in the car, and whizz around until he drops off. This means my hour can't be on the laptop, but I bring a notebook to scribble in, or a draft to correct. Sometimes what I am writing is still so raw that it can be upsetting, but mostly it feels very cathartic to get the things in my head out and down on paper. You might not be a writer, but jotting down your thoughts and feelings might help you feel better in the long run.

6. **I get professional help.** Sometimes this is easier said than done. Don't give up if the first person you reach out to isn't helpful. It's worth noting that I had the resources to pay for my psychologist in Australia. In the UK, NHS provision is patchy and there are long waiting lists. If you don't have the resources to pay while you wait, then I'm afraid it's an extremely hard situation with no easy answer. There are some support organisations listed at the end of this book who may be able to help.

I was extremely lucky with the psychologist I saw, Dr Walker. He has helped me enormously. He has helped me see that some of the bad or negative feelings and emotions I experience have a context in my life, and are not all down to depression. He supported me when I didn't want to take more medication on my return to Sydney, and contradicted the wrong diagnosis. He has helped me to see that I find it difficult to process emotions, and that I tend towards catastrophic thinking.

Earlier this week, after my training session, I went for lunch in a local Forty Beans café. As I munched my way through a tuna mayo and sliced egg sandwich, a family came and sat down next to me at one of the outside tables. There was a woman about my age, with a little baby younger than my son and an older couple I assumed to be her parents.

They were having such a lovely time. The grandparents cooed and doted on the little baby while the mother relaxed with a latte.

I am very homesick after our trip to London, and seeing this group prompted a huge wave of sadness that I was so far away from my family. Before Dr Walker helped me understand about processing my emotions, I would have panicked when I started to feel sad, worrying that my depression was coming back. But, as I now know that I'm vulnerable to feeling a sense of loss when I think about my parents, I just sat there with the feeling, acknowledging it until it ebbed away. Recognition and acceptance lead to other options, as Dr Walker has taught me. Learning to recognise and accept my emotions is part of a lifelong process, and the more I practise, the easier it will get.

I also see Claudette. It was once a week at the beginning, but now it's more like once a month. She has helped me to realise that no one is happy all the time. It seems like such an obvious thing to say, but when she spelled it out to me, I realised I had some very unrealistic ideas about myself and my mood. Some uncomfortable feelings, or sadness, or irritation, are normal parts of life. In fact, we need them, otherwise the good bits wouldn't feel so good. Everything is a balance. Yin and yang again.

7. **I get non-professional help.** It can be so hard to ask, but your friends will probably be aching with sadness for you and will really want to help. My group of friends helped so much by just including me in normal activities, even though I must have been the worst company.

One of the wonderful things my mum did for me was write a record of all the "normal" things I did in the day, which she would read out to me after dinner. I'm not sure why this helped, but it did. Perhaps seeing the achievements written down on paper made them more real? Or maybe she saw how hard I was trying to do things that would be easy for someone not grappling with depression. Perhaps it was a bit of both.

When you are depressed, you really do see the world through a veil of misery and pessimism. It is hard for you to think about, or even remember, anything that doesn't provide evidence to back up the overwhelming feeling that everything is shit, that you are shit, that life is shit.

Mum tells me she was determined to help me see that the real me was still there underneath the layers of depression. She knew it was a monumental struggle for me to take part in normal conversations, but she persevered every day to have light, thoughtful, interesting chats like we've always had. If you are reading this and you have a loved one going through PND, then try to do this with them. Or help them keep a record of their daily achievements. Both really helped me.

8. **I hang out with other people.** Being on my own can make me feel very lonely, so I always try to have plans to meet up with friends and women from my mothers' group every day. The benefits of the company of others still outweighs the tiring surveillance operation that takes place anywhere outside of our child-proofed apartment.

9. **I take my medication.** Enough said. Remember, you have a say about the mix and dose of medication. You need to be happy with it. Also, medication should be taken together with talking therapies. Don't sit back and wait for the medication to kick in. Take an active role in your recovery.

10. **I try to remain positive.** I've put this last because it is the most important thing to try to do, but also the hardest. I try to believe Claudette when she says that all women with postnatal depression get better eventually. I try to believe Kai and my parents when they say that they think I will get better, I just need to give it time. This is very hard to do when you are feeling soul-crushingly awful, but I really try, and I think it is paying off. Try to believe in yourself and your ability to get back to normal.

I've survived my biggest all-encompassing fear: that I would go mad like my sister. That I would be locked up for months on end like she has been, and that the fabric of my life would unravel, that it would be all confusion, pain, and misery.

I did go mad and I survived it. After that, I survived months and months of the grinding misery and anxiety of postnatal depression. Mostly, now, I feel strong both mentally and physically. If and when more bad things happen (as is the case with life), I feel that I will be in a much better position to cope. I survived, and I'm still here to tell the tale.

POSTSCRIPT

It is April 2013. I finished writing a draft of the book three months ago and I've got something to say.

Deep breath.

I'm better. 100% better.

There. I said it.

It feels amazing-yet-scary to actually say that out loud. I sit and wait for the Gods of "Don't Count Your Chickens" to notice my optimism and send me another bolt of depression. But they haven't yet. I think a small part of me will probably always be on the lookout, waiting to see if the depression will return. But mostly, I'm just rejoicing in getting my life back.

Life just seems so *normal*, so easy to cope with, so interesting and fun. I still have times when I feel ratty, stressed, and a bit down. But as Claudette keeps telling me, this is normal. It's a totally normal part of life.

Last night, I sat with my son after he had his milk and I'd finished reading his bedtime story. He is such a wriggler that he doesn't often sit in one place for more than a minute before he wants to be off, running around the room or trying to hit me in the eye with the handle of his maraca. But last night, he snuggled close and babbled softly to me for – oh, about five whole minutes. It was bliss. We sat, me in the chair, him in my lap, and gurgled to each other, his face turned up to mine. I basked in the glow of his soft gaze. He started playing the game of touching my lips.

Every time I kissed his finger, he would smile and laugh – it's the most wonderful sound imaginable, and it enveloped me in such a strong feeling of love and contentment.

I've done it, I thought to myself. *I'm there. I'm better.*

Since finishing the book, things have been steadily improving. At my last meeting with Dr Paul in January, he told me I could start scaling back on the olanzapine (the antipsychotic medication).

'You are officially better,' he declared. 'See, I told you that would happen.'

He gave me a smug, self-satisfied smile. I just looked at him as Kai gave my hand a squeeze.

'That's not what I remember,' I almost said. But I was so happy to be coming off the olanzapine that, in the end, I didn't say anything. What would be the point?

The difference was immediate. I could actually wake up in the morning without the suffocating cloud of permanent tiredness. I started losing weight. My intelligence and quick thinking emerged again. I didn't have any return of symptoms, though I did have a few wobbles (which were more to do with lack of confidence than anything else).

And last week, the marvellous Claudette told me she was discharging me totally from the adult mental health service and handing me over to my GP, who will support me while I decrease the antidepressants. Though I'll really miss Claudette, I am delighted about this. It really is all over.

I was guided through by Kai, my parents, my friends, Claudette, and Dr Walker – though there was one other person who got me through. And that was me.

Life is so hard at times. If you have a period of mental illness, it can completely devastate your life. But my message is not to give up hope.

You are strong, you can cope, and you will get better.

Jen S Wight

POST-POSTSCRIPT

It is December 2018 – the book is just about to be published by Trigger. I am writing this at the desk in my in-laws' kitchen in Fredrikstad, Norway, as the light fades. My family are out in the snow, romping through the pine forest in search of trolls. We moved back to the UK in 2016 to be nearer to family, and though I miss so much about Australia, I'm fundamentally and profoundly glad to be home.

My son is just about to turn seven, and he is a fireball of energy, love, and laughter. One of his favourite things is family hugs, where Kai scoops him up so his face is level with ours and we stand with our arms around each other and take turns kissing each other's cheeks. Don't get me wrong; he is by no means perfect. As I was reading him his bedtime story the other night, he stood up, turned away from me, bent down so his bare bottom was less than three centimetres away from my face, and farted. I could feel the little gust moving air molecules, along with some other molecules I don't want to think about. We had a long conversation about respect that night, let me tell you! But the joy he brings is worth the odd inappropriate blast of methane.

Life doesn't stop with the ending of a chapter; it goes on. Things haven't always gone smoothly since we left Australia. Such lowlights include Kai discovering a brain tumour, which was thankfully removed and found to be non-cancerous, and me having another period of illness.

Women who have experienced postpartum psychosis and / or postnatal depression are at greater risk of subsequent mental ill health. I thought I wouldn't be one of them, but I was.

Being ill again was similar in some ways, but totally different in others. The period of psychosis was much more confused and frightening for me. It came on much quicker after a period of extreme stress had led me to start losing hours and hours of sleep. I was at work on the Thursday, and by Saturday night, locked into a psychiatric ward in Homerton Hospital in Hackney.

One of the things that made it particularly hard was that I admitted myself to a ward in exactly the same hospital my sister had been sectioned into when I was 15. Exactly. The. Same. Hospital.

Enough to send someone crazy, right?

Conversely, what saved me from the realisation that my absolute worst fear was finally coming true (much more so than the relative friendliness of the mother and baby unit in Sydney) was my state of extreme mental confusion. Not being able to string one thought to the next, along with the realisation, deep, deep, down that I was extremely unwell and in need of specialist medical help, protected me from the horror.

I now know that my main two risk factors for getting ill are 1) having a baby and 2) not getting enough sleep. This is invaluable, if painfully won, knowledge.

As much as I didn't enjoy my stay in the mother and baby unit, I now realise how much worse it is in a locked ward. Like before, I only had a week in the ward and discharged myself against medical advice. Like before, the "up" was followed by a "down" of depression, which was more severe but shorter-lived this time.

And, like before, thanks to the help of many and my own guts and determination I recovered completely.

In *Reasons to Stay Alive*, Matt Haig says in response to the truism "What doesn't kill you, makes you stronger' that 'What doesn't kill you very often makes you weaker. What doesn't kill you can leave you limping for the rest of your days. What doesn't kill you can make you scared to leave your house, or even your bedroom, and have you trembling, or mumbling incoherently, or leaning with your head on a window pane, wishing you could return to the time before the thing that didn't kill you."

Someone said to me when I was battling my depression, 'You know you've got better before, you know you can do it again.' This is true in a rational, cold-light-of-day kind of way. But imagine you'd been in a car accident and broken your back, then clawed your way through many months of painful physiotherapy to miraculously walk again. Now imagine that two years later you were in another accident and broke your back again.

As you lie in hospital, flat on your back, whacked out on pain meds, only vaguely aware of the concerned faces of your husband and parents around your bed, you might be comforted by the thought that you'd learnt to walk before in very similar circumstances. But you might think, as I did, *what the fuck?! This again?! What have I done to deserve this?* You might worry, as I did, that it happening twice might somehow reduce the chance of a full recovery. That the second break might permanently damage the scar tissue of the first, making full recovery impossible. You might think, *Recovering fully from a broken back twice? Now, that's never going to happen!*

Imagine that one of the symptoms of a broken back is the fundamental, unshakeable belief that you are never going to get better. You can imagine how much that is going to help you recover! This was my experience of depression.

But, in coming out of the second illness I realise that in some fundamental way I *did* use that knowledge to give me inner strength. I now use that knowledge to power my choices in life and to make the most of the days of health I am now experiencing. I may get ill a third time. I may not. But one thing is for sure: if it does happen, I'm going to do everything I can to get myself well again.

SUPPORT

If you suspect a friend or a loved one has psychosis, call 999 (UK), 000 (Australia) 911 (USA). It is a medical emergency and needs immediate medical attention.

Beyond the crisis though, if you, or someone you know, is struggling with postnatal depression or postpartum psychosis there are organisations which can help through providing information, support, or signposting to other relevant services. Remember, though, it is vital that you are also in direct contact with a health professional who can give you personalised support.

In the UK

- Mind believes no one should have to face a mental health problem alone. They'll listen, give you support and advice, and fight your corner. And they'll push for a better deal and respect for everyone experiencing a mental health problem. **www.mind.org.uk**

- Action Postpartum Psychosis is a network of women across the UK and further afield who have experienced PPP. It is a collaborative project run by women who have experienced PPP and academic experts from Birmingham and Cardiff Universities. **www.app-network.org**

- SANE works to raise mental health awareness, combat stigma, and increase understanding, provide emotional support, practical help and information, and initiate research into causes, treatments, and experiences of mental illness.

www.sane.org.uk
0845 767 8000 –12pm to 2am, every day
including Christmas Day.

In Australia

- The Black Dog Institute is a world leader in the diagnosis, treatment, and prevention of mood disorders such as depression and bipolar disorder.
www.blackdoginstitute.org.au

- The Gidget Foundation is a not-for-profit organisation whose mission is to promote awareness of perinatal anxiety and depression among women and their families, their healthcare providers, and the wider community to ensure that women in need receive timely, appropriate, and supportive care.
www.gidgetfoundation.com.au

- Lifeline provides access to crisis support, suicide prevention, and mental health support services. 13 11 14
www.lifeline.org.au

- beyondblue is a national, independent, not-for-profit organisation working to address issues associated with depression, anxiety and related disorders in Australia.
www.beyondblue.org.au

- MotherSafe provides a comprehensive counselling service for women and their healthcare providers concerned about exposures during pregnancy and breastfeeding. Such exposures may include: prescription drugs, over-the-counter medications, street drugs, infections, radiation, or occupational exposures. www.mothersafe.org.au

BIBLIOGRAPHY

Carroll, L. and Tenniel, J. (2012). *Alice's Adventures in Wonderland: And, Through the Looking Glass*. London: Vintage, p.245.

Cusk, R. (2014). *A Life's Work*. London: Faber & Faber, p.4.

Haig, M. (2015). *Reasons to Stay Alive*. London: Canongate Books, p.122.

ACKNOWLEDGEMENTS

Thank you:

To my friends and work colleagues in Sydney and London for all your love and support, whether it was not flinching as I described my pain while we sat in Clissold Park, or joining me on trips to Taronga Zoo, or making me homemade gazpacho, and most of all for still treating me like *me* when I felt so lost.

To almost all the mental health professionals I've met since I've been ill. You do a very tough job with some of the most vulnerable people in our society. Thank you so much. My journey would have been much longer and much harder without you.

To my neighbours in Sydney, John and Gabriella, who gave my mum a room to sleep in while she was with us for six weeks at the height of my depression, and who stopped me smashing my bedroom window and instead called the emergency locksmith when I managed to get myself locked out of the flat with my son inside.

To my advance readers Hannah, Bhavna, Susannah and Hilary, whose comments and encouragement spurred me on to finish the book – I can't say how much it meant to me. And a special thank you to Hilary for her detailed proofreading and for always campaigning my writing.

To Susannah M, The Bunce and Bill for their encouragement, inspiration and wonderful teaching during my MA in Professional Writing at University College Falmouth.

To my agent, Charlotte at Kingsford Campbell, for championing my story and being so lovely.

To the whole team at Trigger for their eagle-eyed editing, creativity and expertise. Special thanks to Katie and Chris for working with me to improve the MS with such patience and tact.

To my wonderful pal, Catherine, for doing the impossible and actually taking a nice picture of me for my author photo.

To Kai's parents for their loving care and concern.

To my sister, Tania, for her kindness, love, and curry when I needed it.

To my parents, who raised me to never give up and who have never doubted me. I felt your unwavering support every day, even when we were half the planet away from each other and even more so now that we are just across Clissold Park.

A special thank you to my amazing mum who dropped everything and flew halfway around the world to care for me and my son while I fought my way out of my depression. You will never know just how much I appreciate what you did and have always done for me.

To my little big sister, whose courage and determination has always inspired me. And the parcels and postcards – little reminders of love and care and thought. I love you, Sis.

To Kai for always being there, even when "there" was a shitty place to be. I will never forget how you stood by me, practically and emotionally, through all the bad times.

To my son, the little package of wonder, for your energy and love and for bringing so much light and joy into my life.

If you found this book interesting ...
why not read these next?

Postpartum Depression and Anxiety

The Definitive Treatment and Recovery Approach

A refreshing, compassionate and user-friendly
self-help book to guide and support parents experiencing
postpartum depression and anxiety.

Daddy Blues

Postnatal Depression and Fatherhood

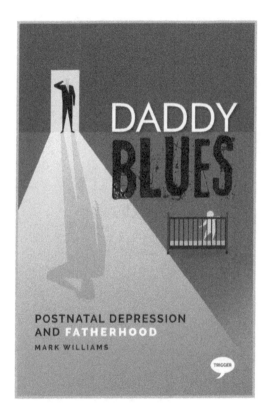

Mark knew of baby blues for mothers, but never thought it might happen to him. And then it did. *Daddy Blues* explores a story we all know, from a different perspective.

When the Bough Breaks

The Pursuit of Motherhood

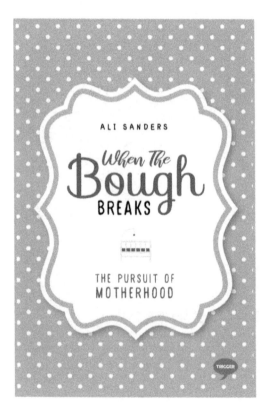

Motherhood was all Ali Sanders had ever wanted out of life.
She just didn't expect it to be such a rocky road to happiness.

the *Shaw* **mind**
FOUNDATION

Creating hope for children,
adults and families

Sign up to our charity, The Shaw Mind Foundation
www.shawmindfoundation.org
and keep in touch with us; we would love to hear
from you.

*We aim to bring to an end the suffering and despair caused
by mental health issues. Our goal is to make help and support
available for every single person in society, from all walks of
life. We will never stop offering hope. These are our promises.*

TRIGGER™
The mental health & wellbeing publisher

www.triggerpublishing.com

Trigger is a publishing house devoted to opening conversations about mental health. We tell the stories of people who have suffered from mental illnesses and recovered, so that others may learn from them.

Adam Shaw is a worldwide mental health advocate and philanthropist. Now in recovery from mental health issues, he is committed to helping others suffering from debilitating mental health issues through the global charity he co-founded, The Shaw Mind Foundation. www.shawmindfoundation.org

Lauren Callaghan (CPsychol, PGDipClinPsych, PgCert, MA (hons), LLB (hons), BA), born and educated in New Zealand, is an innovative industry-leading psychologist based in London, United Kingdom. Lauren has worked with children and young people, and their families, in a number of clinical settings providing evidence based treatments for a range of illnesses, including anxiety and obsessional problems. She was a psychologist at the specialist national treatment centres for severe obsessional problems in the UK and is renowned as an expert in the field of mental health, recognised for diagnosing and successfully treating OCD and anxiety related illnesses in particular. In addition to appearing as a treating clinician in the critically acclaimed and BAFTA award-winning documentary *Bedlam*, Lauren is a frequent guest speaker on mental health conditions in the media and at academic conferences. Lauren also acts as a guest lecturer and honorary researcher at the Institute of Psychiatry Kings College, UCL.